101

PHOTOSHOP

Hidden Gems and Tips & Tricks

Victoria Pavlov

Published by Victoria Pavlov

Copyright ©2017 by Victoria Pavlov

TRADEMARKS
All terms mentioned in this book that are known to be trademarks or service marks have been appropriately capitalized. Victoria Pavlov cannot attest to the accuracy of this information. Use of a term in the book should not be regarded as affecting the validity of any trademark or service mark.

WARNING AND DISCLAIMER
This book is designed to provide information about Adobe™ Photoshop®. Every effort has been made to make this book as complete and as accurate as possible, but no warranty of fitness is implied.
The information is provided on an as-is basis. The author shall have neither liability nor responsibility to any person or entity with respect to any loss or damages arising from the information contained in this book.

www.pavlovphotography.com

This book is dedicated to Kalebra Kelby because you always inspire to do better and to Terry White because you always encourage me to be positive and enjoy life.

About the Author

Victoria Pavlov

Artist, Photographer, Digital Painter, Designer
I was born in musical family and started practicing music at age 3. I was practicing for about 5 hours every day but this did not stop me from starting to draw at age7. My first type of drawing (and still my favorite) was portrait. At age 15 I had my first big exhibition where I was surprised (as any child would be) of all "WOWs" I heard from the people attending.

The first time I was Introduced to photography was at age 8 when I saw my uncle's camera and his work it inspired me to see how different photography and painting could be. All my life, from an early childhood my primary subject has been people and the human eye. I believe that eyes are the window to the human soul. I always ask my models to show me their personality during the shoot. I am not looking for a pretty face I am looking for a person's personality. Because of my artistic background my photography is telling a story with images. The technical aspect in my photography is very important to me, especially when it comes to lighting. I don't like any shadows on my subjects unless I do it on purpose. I spent about two years to find the lightning technique that I love and am happy with.

I was introduced to Adobe Photoshop version 1.0. And since that time Photoshop has become my everything, my soul, my method of communication, my method to express myself. I am always saying " Nothing is impossible with Photoshop". My work in Photoshop includes everything from photo retouching, web design and image manipulation to digital painting. This is a very special world to me.

I truly believe that with Adobe Photoshop we can make this world more beautiful and less violent.

Contents

Introduction

I wanted to write a book that every Photoshop user could learn from. Many of us are new to Photoshop, use it regularly or are experts. However, no matter what your Photoshop skill level is, chances are you can still learn new things or pick up tips from this book that you haven't discovered yet. My editor said "wow, I learned at least 10 things right off the bat that I didn't know and I'm not done editing yet." We get into our groove and we use the same features and techniques all the time. However, with each new update to Photoshop CC there are usually little things that the engineers at Adobe add or change that often don't get a mention. I did my best to pick out 101 of my favorites. Enjoy!

#1 Layers Panel
Add "copy" to copied layers and groups

Organization in Adobe Photoshop is very important to me. I like to have all of my panels arranged in a specific position, My toolbar displays tools that I need in the workspace I am currently working in. I like to apply colored labels to my layers and menus and to be able to add "copy" to duplicated layers. I also group my layers making my workflow less stressful and more enjoyable.

When you duplicate layers or groups Adobe Photoshop adds "copy" to the duplicated layer(s) or groups.

Click on the drop down menu (on the top right of the Layers panel) > Select "Panel Options" (image1)

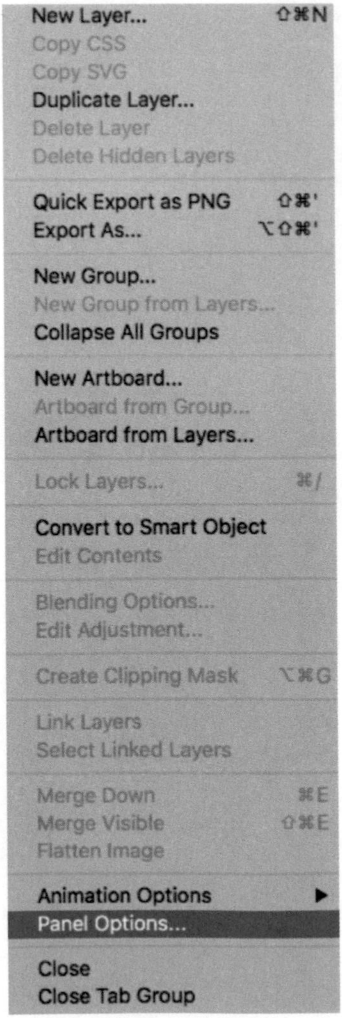

image 1

Check "Add "copy" to Copied Layers and Groups (images 2, 2.1 and 2.2)

image 2

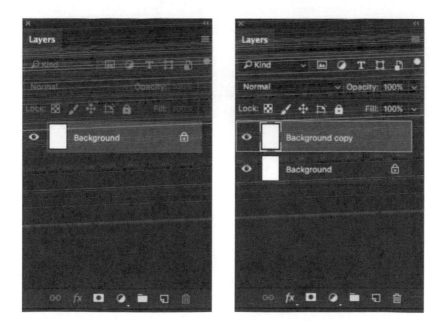

image 2.1   *image 2.2*

#2 Show/hide Layer Styles/Effects in the Layers Panel

In Adobe Photoshop CC you can add a non-destructive layer style to any layer. I am using layer styles all the time and I love them. The best part is that I can show or hide the list of applied layer style(s). For example, if I have more than 10 layers (I usually have more) and after the 9th layer I want to apply the same layer style I applied to layer 3 to my new layer (or if you want to modify a previously applied style) I'll need to be able to see the ones I applied. To be able to see which layer styles I've used I always have the Expand New Effects enabled. If you turn this off, styles and effects can be applied but you'll have to manually expand the list to see them.
Click on the dropdown menu (on the top right of the Layers panel) > Select "Panel Options" (image3)

image 3

New Layer...	⇧⌘N
Copy CSS	
Copy SVG	
Duplicate Layer...	
Delete Layer	
Delete Hidden Layers	
Quick Export as PNG	⇧⌘'
Export As...	⌥⇧⌘'
New Group...	
New Group from Layers...	
Collapse All Groups	
New Artboard...	
Artboard from Group...	
Artboard from Layers...	
Lock Layers...	⌘/
Convert to Smart Object	
Edit Contents	
Blending Options...	
Edit Adjustment...	
Create Clipping Mask	⌥⌘G
Link Layers	
Select Linked Layers	
Merge Down	⌘E
Merge Visible	⇧⌘E
Flatten Image	
Animation Options	▶
Panel Options...	
Close	
Close Tab Group	

Check "Expand new Effects" (image 4 and 4.1)

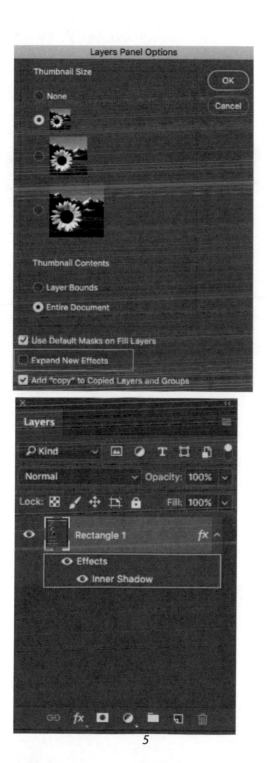

image 4

image 4.1

#3 Turn on/off the Layers Panel Search Option

After a few hours working on a project and 15 layers later the Layer Search Bar can be a helpful feature. I can filter my search by "filter for pixel layers", "filter for adjustment layers", "filter for type layers", "filter for shape layers", "filter for smart objects". So even if you don't remember the name of your layers you can still do searches. (image 5)

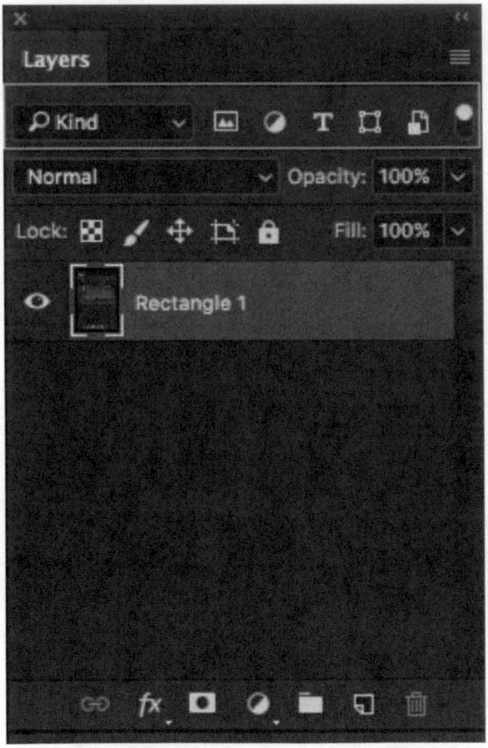

image 5

You can turn The Layer filtering off (image 6) or on (image 7)
) or off (image 8)

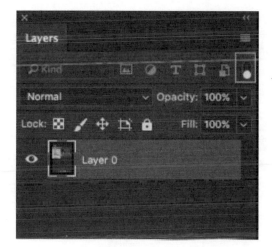

image 6

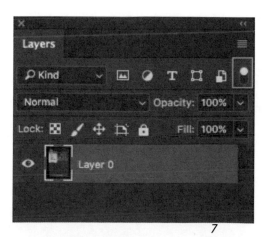

image 7

#4 Search Layers by name

You can use other great search (or filter) layer options. You can search for a layer by:
Kind
Name
Effect
Mode
Attribute
Color
Smart Object
Selected
Artboard

Simply choose any criteria from drop down menu (image 8)

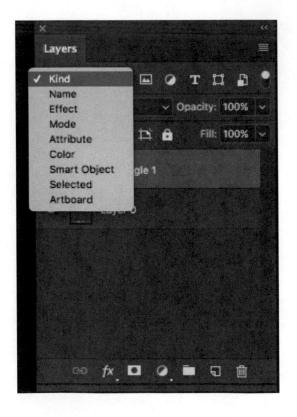

image 8

#5 Arranging Layers from the Keyboard

When working on my compositing or design projects having the ability to arrange my layers is very important. I would say that the ability to arrange my layers is the key to the right composition.

To move Layers Up or Down:

Select Layer(s) > hold Command(Mac) / Ctrl(Win) and use right and left bracket keys " [or] ". You cant move up or down background layer before you will unlock it)

Move up (image 9)

Move down (image10)

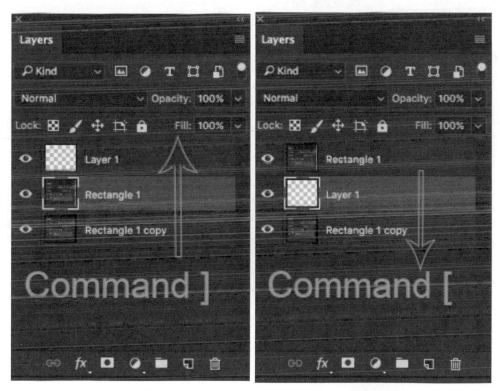

image 9   image 10

#6 To move a layer to top or to bottom of your layers panel

To bring a layer to the top:
Press > Command + Shift +] (Mac) or Ctrl+Shift+](Win) (image11)

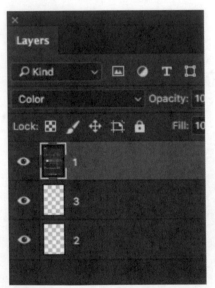

image 11

To move a layer to the bottom:
Press > Command+Shift+[(Mac) or Ctrl+Shift+[(Win) (image 12)

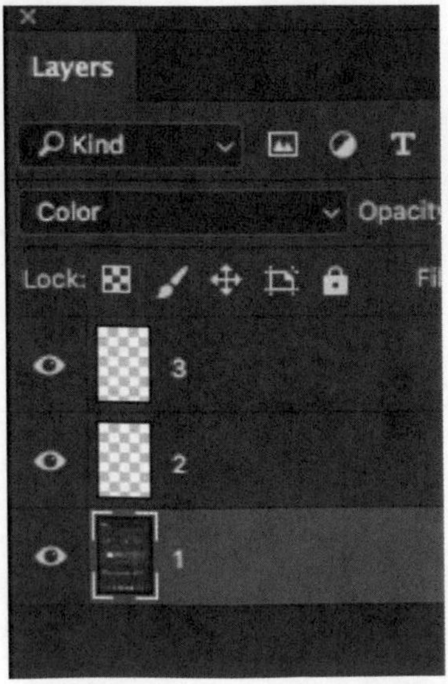

image12

#7 Select a layer without touching your mouse

The ability to select any layer without single mouse click is one of the best Adobe Photoshop features.
To select any Layer:
Press > Option +] or [(Mac) or Alt +] or [(Win) (image 13)

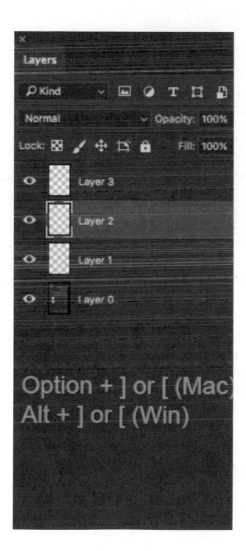

image 13

#8 Selecting multiple Layers at once

Very often I need to select multiple layers. Select the first Layer > press Shift > click on any other layer. All layers in-between the first and the last selected will be selected at the same time (image 14)

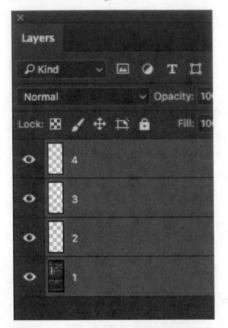

image 14

To add multiple Layers to the selected Layer:
Select the first Layer > press Command (Mac) or Ctrl (Win) > click on each Layer you want to add individually (image 15)

image 15

#9 Create a Layer Group

Creating Layers group makes it easier to work with affect multiple layers at the same time. When I am working in my painting projects I have more than 150 layers on average. After 15 layers I don't always remember which layer is which (even when I am renaming them it's very difficult to remember all of them). To be more organized and spend less time looking for specific layers I create Layers Groups. For example, I would create a "hair" group with all my "hair" layers (note: even inside the Layers group, don't forget to name your Layers). Later when I need to come back and continue working on my subject's hair I will simply expend my "Hair" group and easily find all necessary Layers I want to work with).

To create a Layer group:
 #1 Select all layers you want to create a group with > drag those Layers to Group icon or Click the Group Icon and name the group (image16)

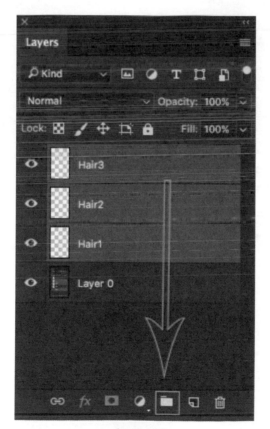

image 16

#2: Select all Layers you want to create a group with > right click > Group from Layers (image17)

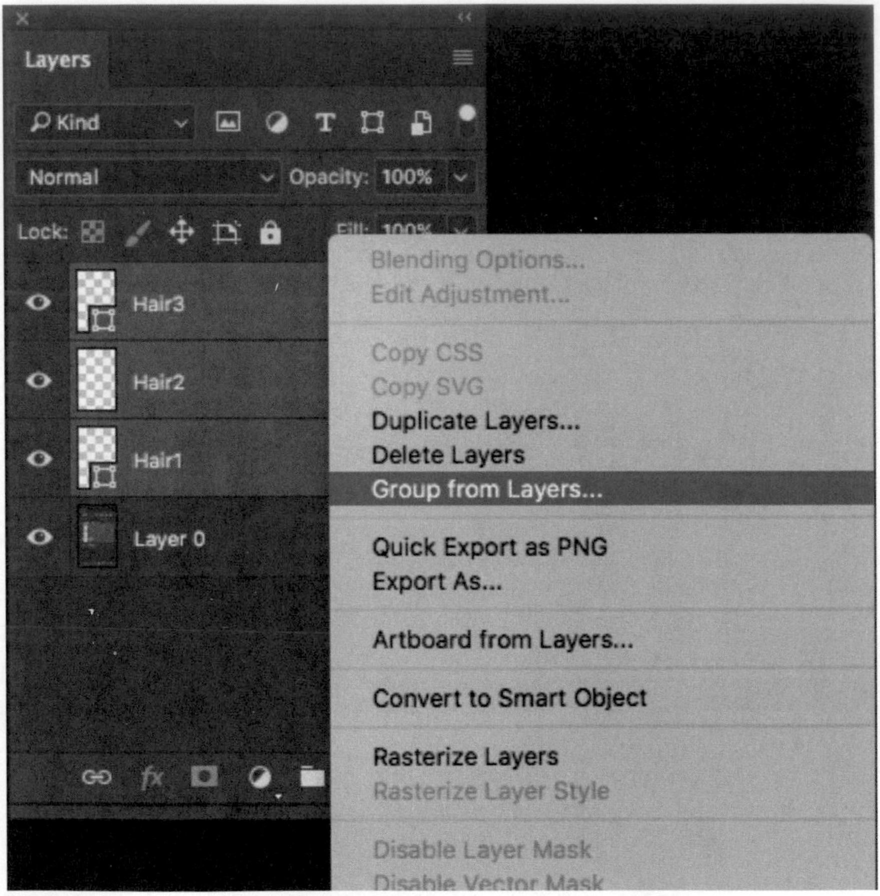

image 17

#3: Click on Create a New Group > drag all layers you want to have into the Group folder (image 18)

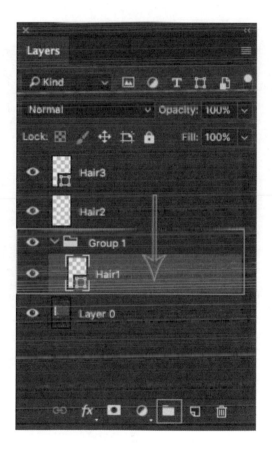

image 18

#4: Select all layers you want to create a group from > press Command +G (Mac) or Ctrl +G (Win)

#10 Turn on/off visibility of multiple Layers at once

Often when working in Photoshop I like to preview a specific Layer separately. To preview only one layer I need to turn visibility of rest of the Layers off.
To turn visibility of all layers except the selected one:
Select Layer > press Option (Mac) or Alt (Win) and click on selected Layer visibility icon (images19 and 19.1)

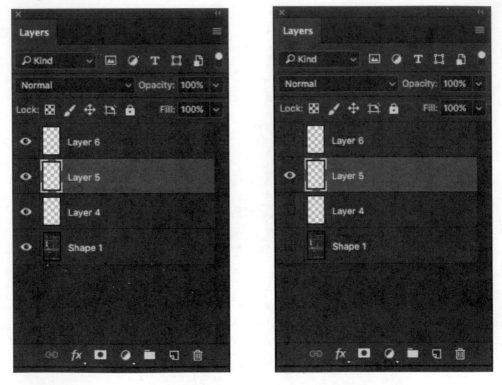

image 19   image 19.1

To turn visibility of all layers back on:
press Option (Mac) or Alt (Win) and click on selected Layer visibility icon.

Tip: to hide visibility of many layers just click and drag down the visibility column

#11 Create a new layer below the selected layer

Its very easy to create a new Layer below the selected layer.
Simply select the Layer that you want the new layer to be under and press Command (Mac) or Ctrl (Win) > click on Create a New Layer icon (images 20 and 20.1)

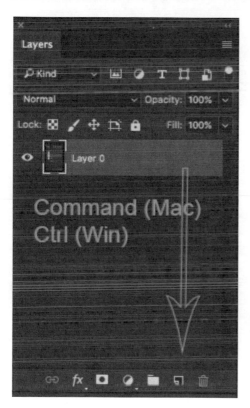

image 20

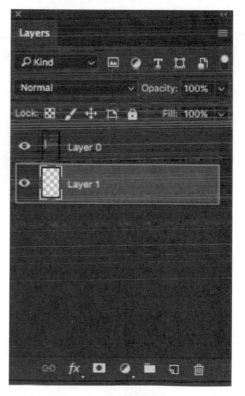

image 20.1

#12 Create a new Layer

To create a new Layer:
press Command + Shift + N (Mac) or Ctrl + Shift +N (Win) (image 21)

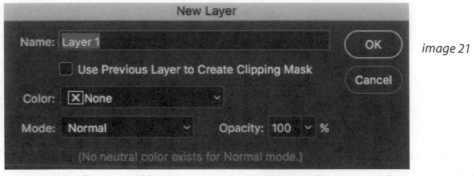

image 21

#13 Select all Layers except the Background (locked) Layer

To select all Layers except the Background (locked) Layer:
press Command + Option + A (Mac) or Ctrl + Alt +A (Win) (image 22)

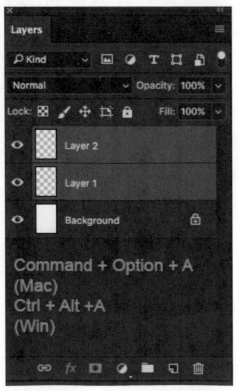

image 22

#14 Move the layer style

I lost count of how many times I've applied a layer style to the wrong Layer by mistake. Next time don't undo. Just move it to the intended layer.
To move the style from one Layer to another:
press Shift > click on a Layer style > drag (Mac) or Ctrl > click on a Layer style > drag (Win) (images 23 and 23.1)

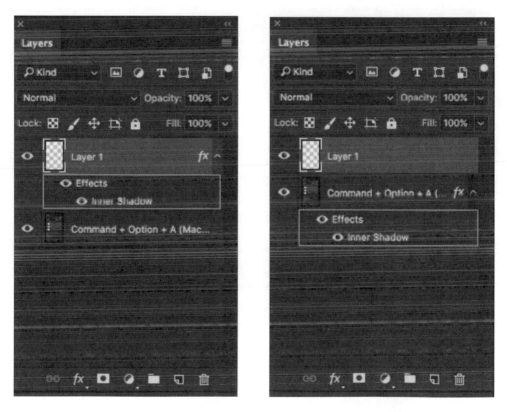

image 23   image 23.1

#15 Copy a Layers Style to Another Layer

To copy the style from one Layer to another:
press Option (Mac) or Alt (Win) > click on the style > drag to another Layer.

#16 Copy the styles from one Layer to multiple Layers

In my graphic design workflow I often apply the same style to multiple Layers (especially in my logo design workflow).
To copy the styles from one Layer to multiple Layers:
Right Click on the style icon and choose Copy Layer Style (image 24)

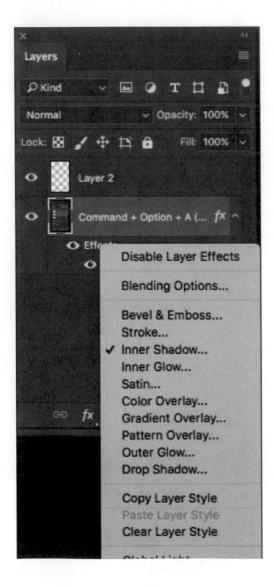

image 24

Select Layers you want to apply the copied style right click again and choose Paste
Layer Style (image 25)

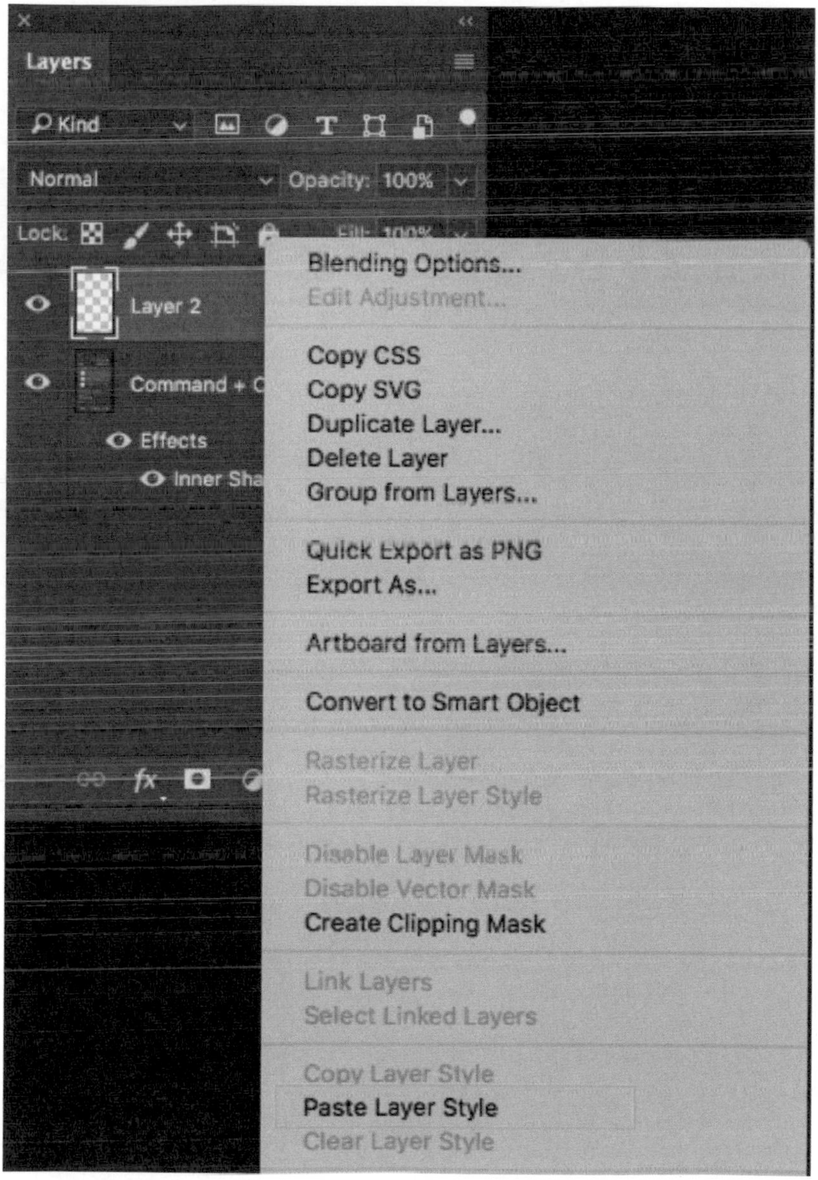

image 25

#17 Add a Layer without Options

To add the empty Layer without any options simply:
press Command + Shift + Option + N (Mac) or Crtl + Shift + Alt + N (Win)

#18 Move and Select Layers Shortcuts

Move Layer Up: Command +] (Mac) or Ctrl +] (Win)
Move Layer Down: Command +[(Mac) or Ctrl + [(Win)
Move Layer All the Way Up: Command + Shift +] (Mac) or Ctrl + Shift +] (Win)
Move Layer All the Way Down: Command + Shift + [(Mac) or Ctrl + Shift + [(Win)
Select All Layers: Command + Option +A (Mac) or Ctrl + Alt + A (Win)

#19 Merge Layers Shortcuts

Merge Layers: Command+ E (Mac) or Ctrl + E (Win)
Merge Layers to New Layer: Command + Option + E (Mac) or Ctrl + Alt + E (Win)
Merge Visible: Command + Shift + E (Mac) or Ctrl + Shift + E (Win)
Merge All Visible to New Layer: Command + Shift + Option + E (Mac) or Ctrl + Shift + Alt + E (Win)

#20 A few very helpful Layer shortcuts

Show/Hide Layers Panel: F7
Duplicate Layer or Selection to New Layer: Command + J (Mac) or Ctrl + J (Win)
Active Selection from Layer: Command + Click on Layer Preview (Mac) or Ctrl + Click on Layer Preview (Win)

#21 Blending Modes Shortcuts

Blending Modes are one of my absolutely favorite features in Adobe Photoshop CC. Using shortcuts saving a lot of time and significantly help in my workflow. I can't imagine to use "manual" method to cycle thought blending modes.
Bellow I listed bunch of shortcuts that will change your life:

Shift + Minus (cycle Up) or Shift-Plus (cycle Down)
Shift + Option + N (Mac) or Shift + Alt + N (Win): Normal
Shift + Option + I(Mac) or Shift + Alt + I: Dissolve
————————————————
Shift + Option + Q (Mac) or Shift + Alt + Q (Win) : Darken
Shift + Option + R (Mac) or Shift + Alt + R (Win): Multiply
Shift + Option + K (Mac) or Shift + Alt + K (Win): Color Burn
Shift + Option + M(Mac) or Shift + Alt + M (Win): Linear Burn
Shift + Option + B (Mac) or Shift + Alt + B (Win) : Darker Color
————————————————
Shift + Option + A (Mac) or Shift + Alt + A (Win): Lighten
Shift + Option + G (Mac) or Shift + Alt + G (Win): Screen
Shift + Option + S (Mac) or Shift + Alt + S (Win): Color Dodge
Shift + Option + D (Mac) or Shift + Alt + D (Win): Linear Dodge
Shift + Option I W (Mac) or Shift + Alt + W (Win): Lighter Color
————————————————
Shift + Option + O (Mac) or Shift + Alt + O (Win): Overlay
Shift + Option + F (Mac) or Shift + Alt + F (Win): Soft Light
Shift + Option + H (Mac) or Shift + Alt + H (Win): Hard Light
Shift + Option + V (Mac) or Shift + Alt + V (Win): Vivid Light
Shift + Option + J (Mac) or Shift + Alt + J (Win): Linear Light
Shift + Option + Z (Mac) or Shift I Alt I Z (Win): Pin Light
Shift + Option + L (Mac) or Shift + Alt + L (Win): Hard Mix
————————————————
Shift + Option + E (Mac) or Shift + Alt + E (Win): Difference
Shift + Option + X (Mac) or Shift + Alt + X (Win): Exclusion
————————————————
Shift + Option +U (Mac) or Shift + Alt + U (Win): Hue
Shift + Option + T (Mac) or Shift + Alt + T (Win): Saturation
Shift + Option + C (Mac) or Shift + Alt + C (Win): Color
Shift + Option + Y (Mac) or Shift + Alt + Y (Win): Luminosity

#22 Create a Smart Object when Placing an Image

Smart objects are a very important part of my workflow. A Smart Object is layer that contain all data from vector or raster images but in a protected wrapper. Working with smart objects helps you apply nondestructive editing such as nondestructive:
Transforms
Filters
Layer Masks
and more.

To speed up your entire nondestructive workflow simply check "Always Create Smart Objects when Placing". When you check this box Adobe Photoshop automatically create a smart objects during your image placement.

Preferences > General > Always Create Smart Objects when Placing (image 26)

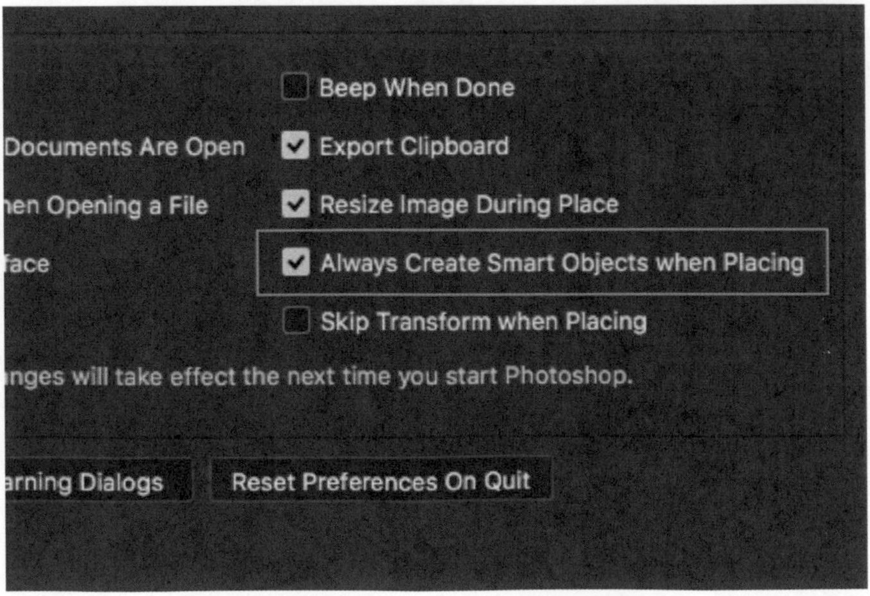

Beep When Done

Documents Are Open   ☑ Export Clipboard

en Opening a File   ☑ Resize Image During Place

ace   ☑ Always Create Smart Objects when Placing

                           ☐ Skip Transform when Placing

nges will take effect the next time you start Photoshop.

arning Dialogs   Reset Preferences On Quit

image 26

#23 Menus Colors

Adobe Photoshop allows us to customize your Photoshop interface in many ways. One option to customize Photoshop is to add Customize Menus Colors. Personally I prefer to apply custom color to my menus. I am a visual person and visual representation is a big factor to me. I customize my menus as a way to have better organization.
Example: I applied green to Save menu. Why Green for the Save menu? Because green color associated with "good to go".
I used Red on the "Close" menu command. Why red? because when I will see the red color I will think twice before I click on that menu item. Red is usually associated with "Stop and think".
You can apply color to menu by:

#1: choosing Edit > Menus (image 27)

image 27

In Keyboard Shortcuts and Menus click on each menu you want to apply color and choose a color from drop down menu (images 28, 28.1 and 28.2

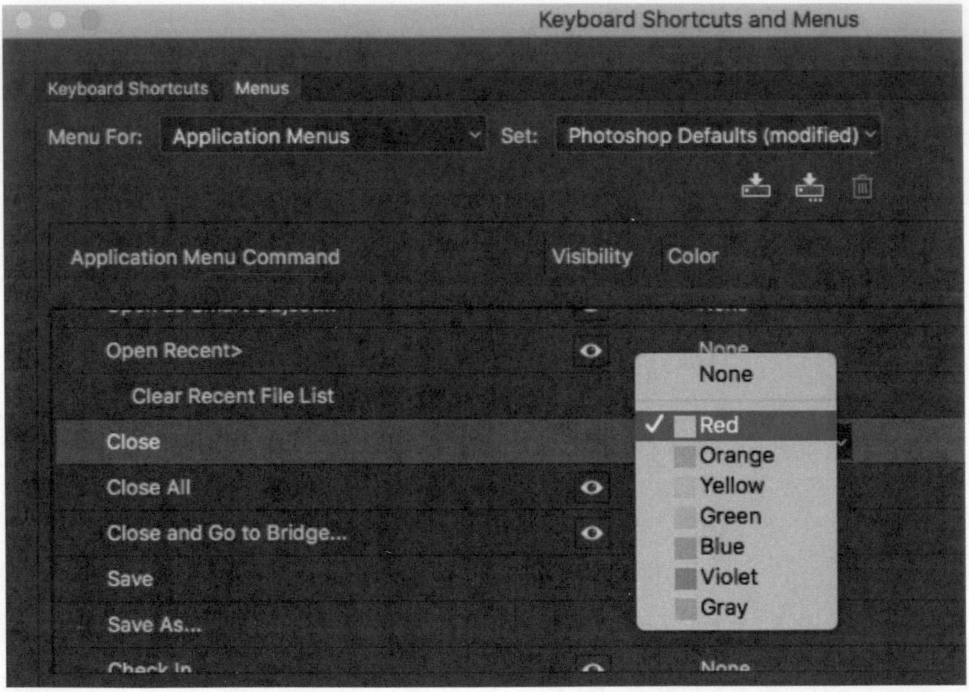

image 28

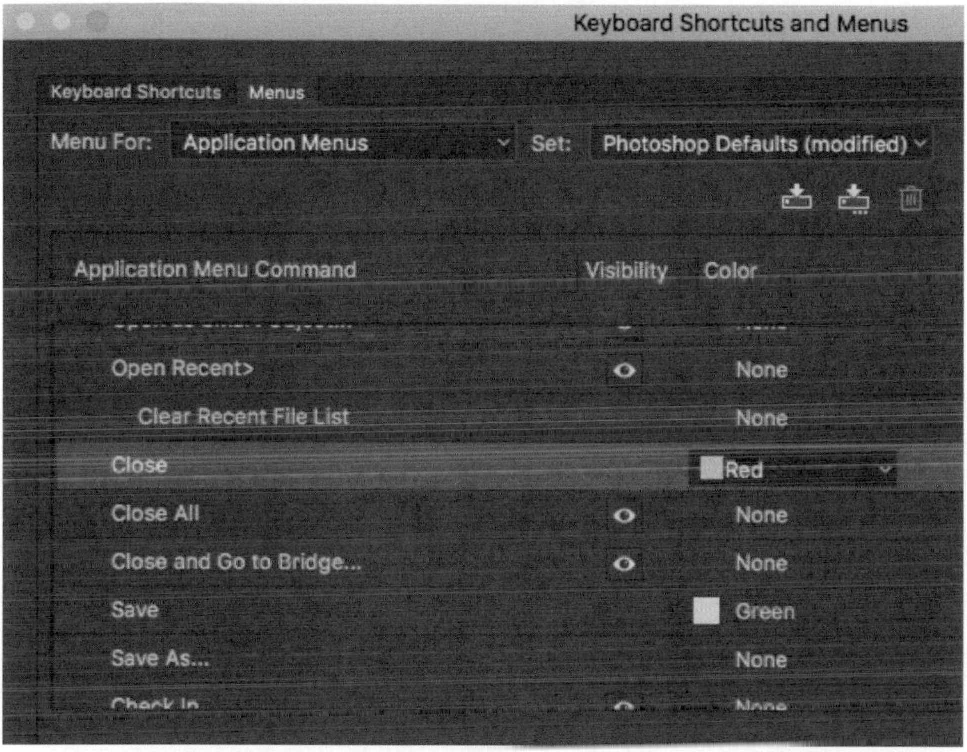

image 28.1

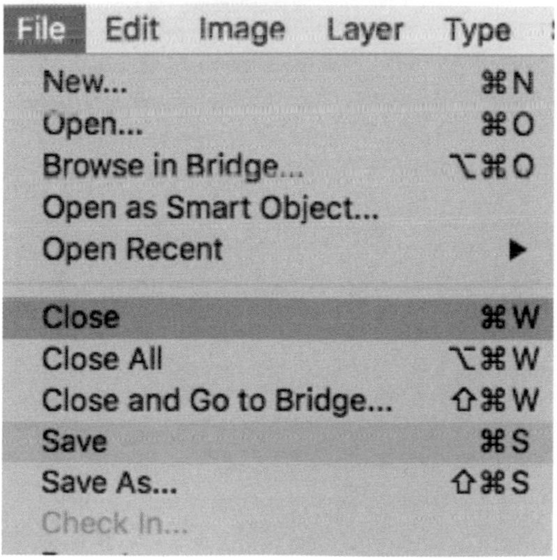

image 28.2

Tip: Check "Show Menu Color" Box
Preferences > Interface > Check "Show Menu Color" box (image29)

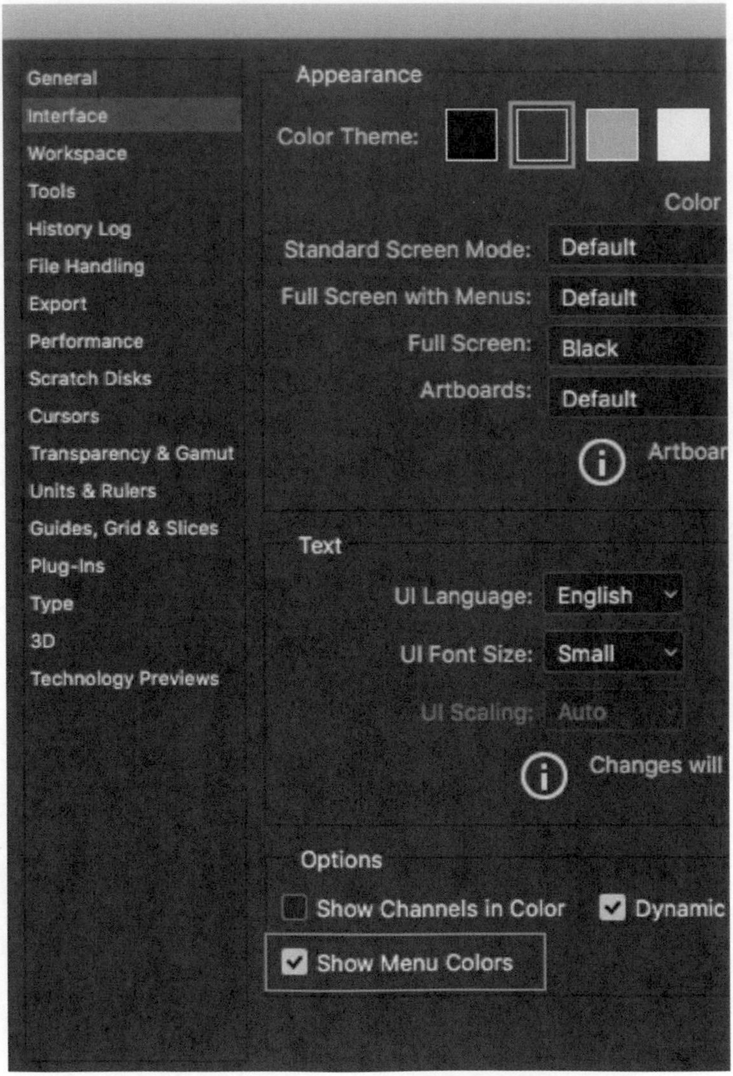

image 28

#24 Open Documents as a tab

When I work on a project and I have many documents open at the same time I prefer to have to my documents opened as tabs. It will save me space in Photoshop's interface and easy to navigate between my opened documents.
To enable floating document window docking:
Preferences > Workspace > check "Enable Floating Document Window Docking" box (image 29)

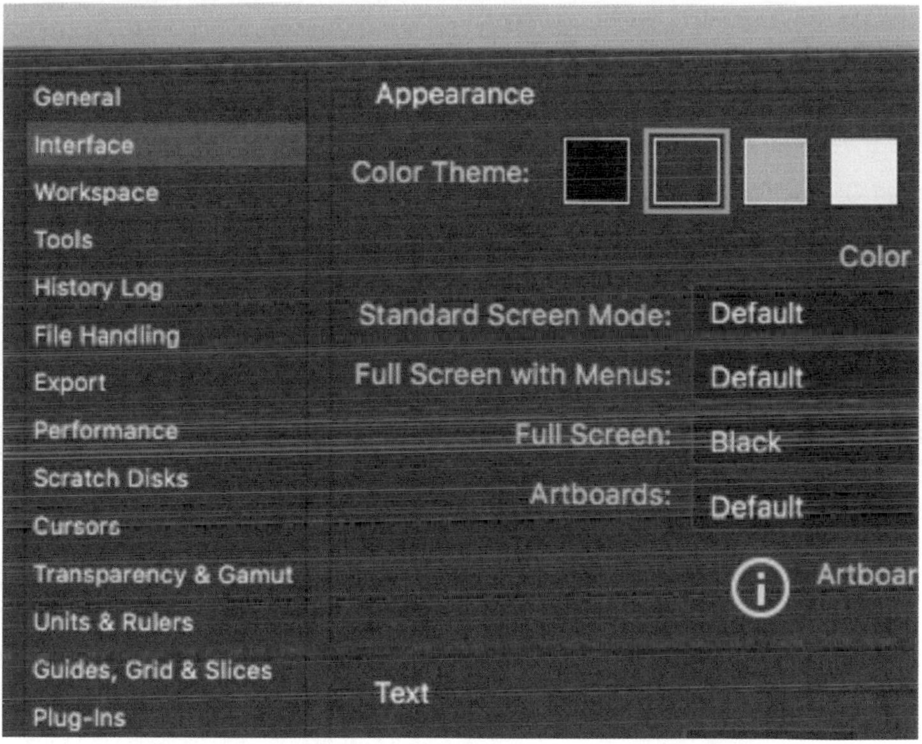

image 29

#25 Layer Masks to Select and Mask Shortcut

Select and Mask workspace is a very helpful feature that helps you to improve the entire selecting and masking workflow along with a big timer saving factor.
I do lots of selecting and masking every day so I found this cool little tip that allows me to set the default tool behavior like double-clicking a layer mask opens the Select and Mask workspace and that will save a lot of time and simplify my workflow.
To set the default tool behavior simply:
Preferences > Tools > check " Double Click Layer Mask Launches Select and Mask Workspace (image 30)

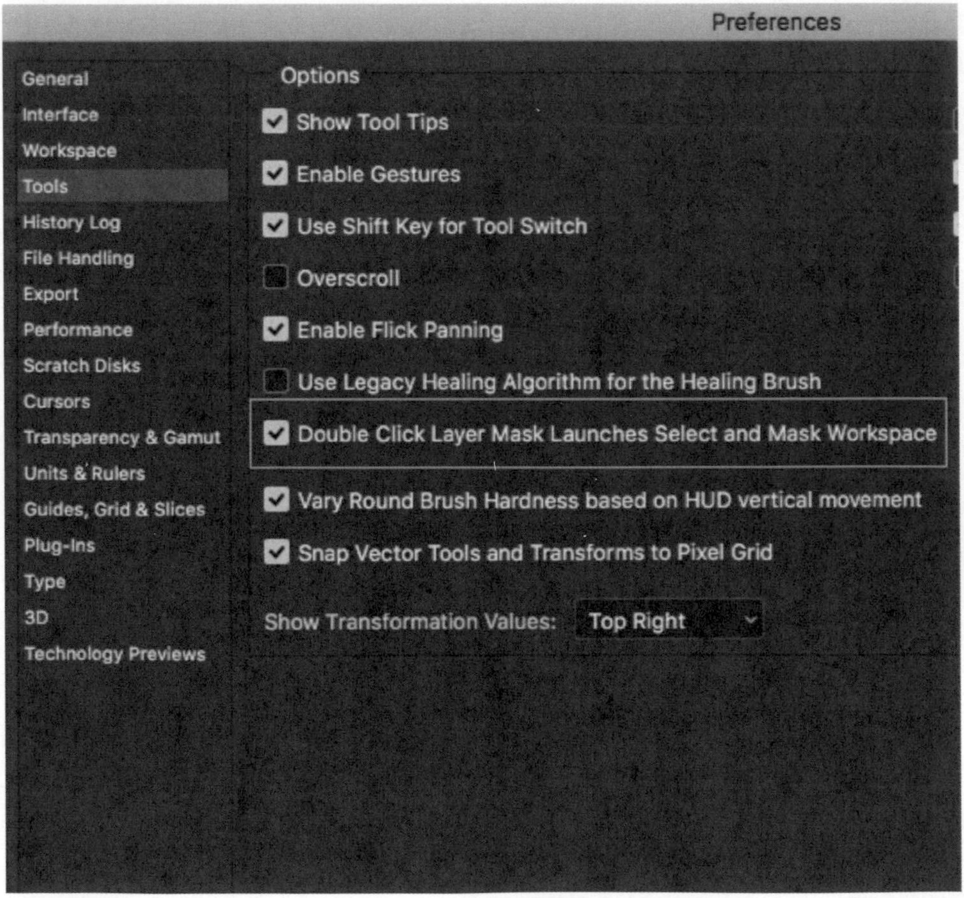

image 30

#26 Don't lose hours of your work!

Setup autosave the right way and it will save you a lot of headache. It's easy and very effective.
Preferences > File Handling > check "Automatically Save Recovery Information Every" box > Choose 5 Minutes (image 31). Photoshop will save document information for recovery every 5 minutes in case you crash. In theory you'd never lose more than 5 minutes of work!

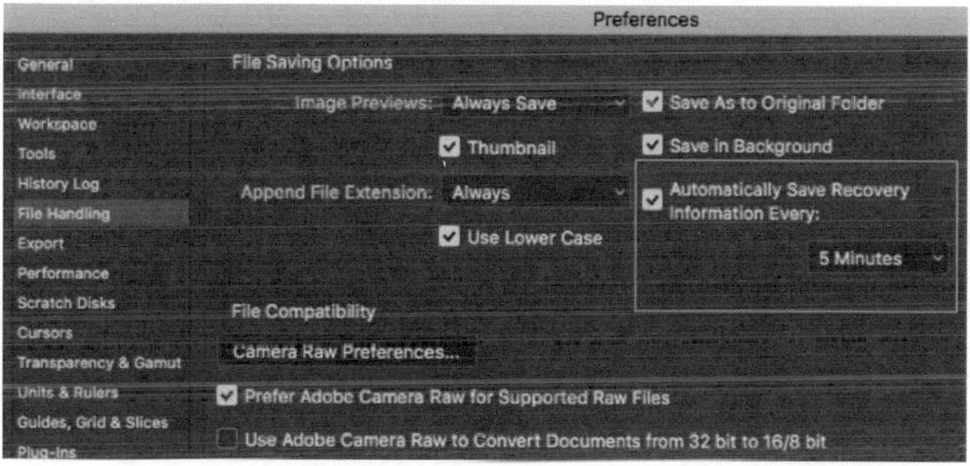

image 31

#27 Save As to original folder

In many cases I prefer to have my document saved to the original document folder. To setup this behavior as a default saves me time.
Preferences > File Handling > check " Save As to Original Folder" box (image 32)

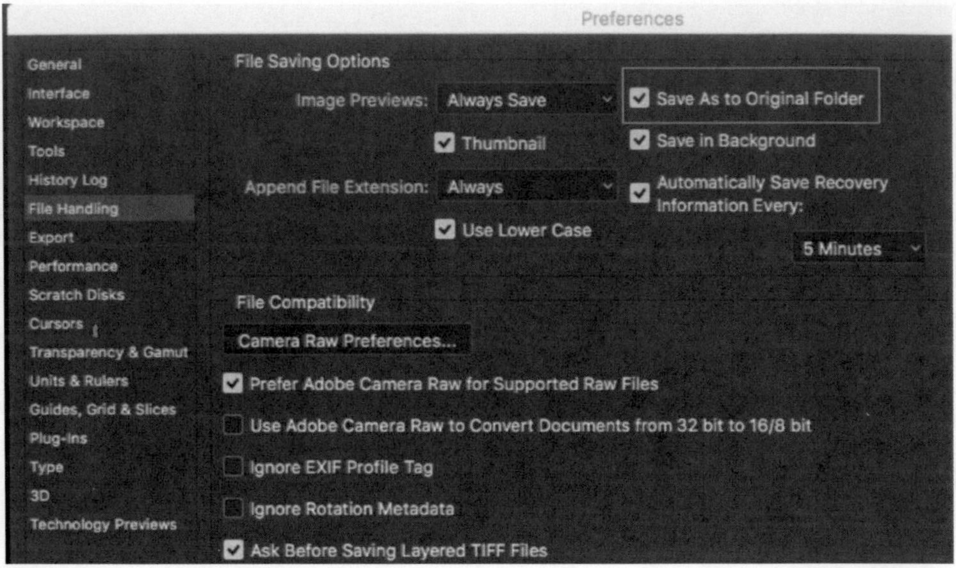

image 32

#28 Quick Export Format Setting

Quick Export is a great option to quickly export the document you're working on to a JPG, PNG, etc. I prefer to have my Quick Export format as PNG.
Preferences > Export > PNG (tip: check "Transparency" box) (image 33)

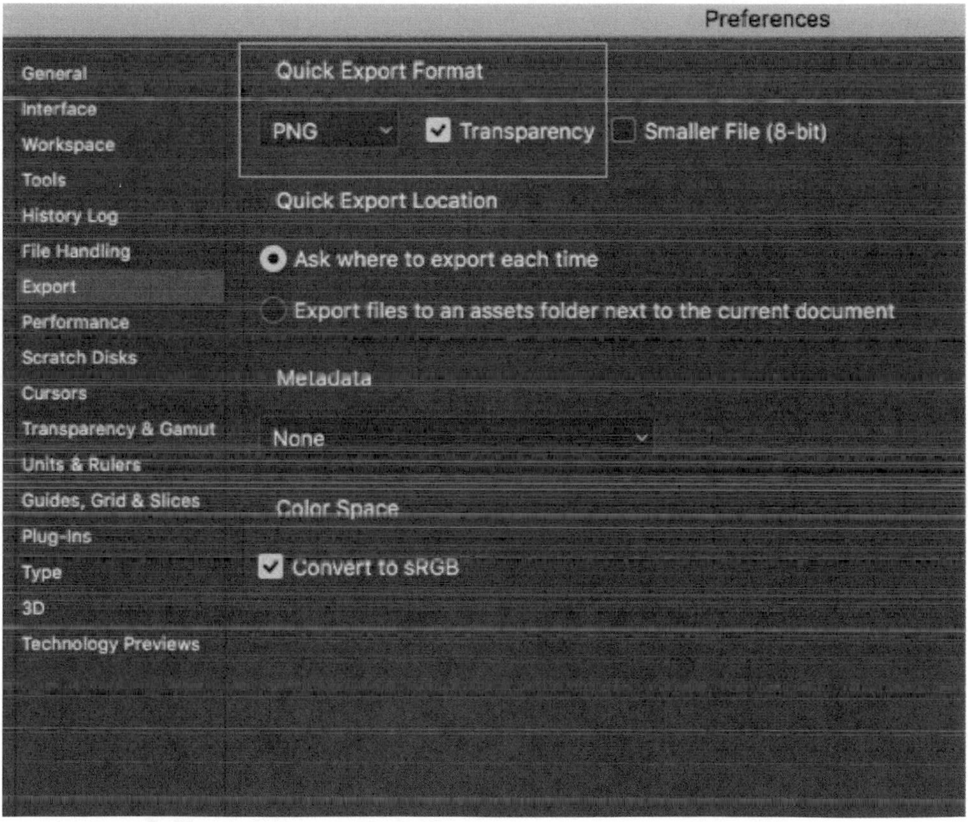

image 33

#29 The History States

I prefer to have setup my History States to 50. Increasing the History States allow you more undos (history states).
Preferences > Performance > Choose 50 from History State drop down menu
(image 34)

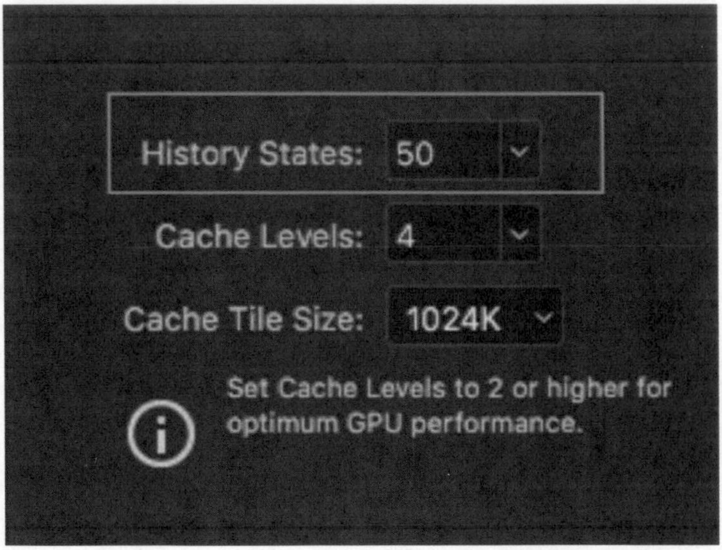

image 34

Tip: The more history states you use the more RAM/scratch disk space is required by Photoshop

#30 Customize your Cursors

My favorite Cursors settings:
Painting Cursors: Full Size Brush Tip
Other Cursors: Standard
Brush Preview Color: I prefer to have it in a dark red
Preferences > Cursors
(image 35)

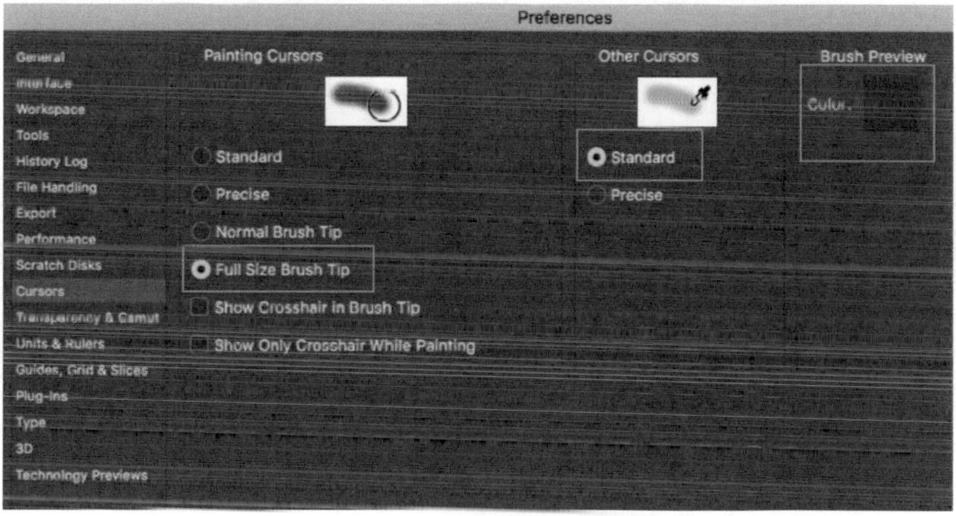

image 35

#31 Customize your Guides, Grid, Slices Preferences

Adobe Photoshop allows you to customize guides, grid, and slices. After spending many hours working in Photoshop you will find that the right setup helps with your productivity and makes your workflow more enjoyable.
Preferences > Guides, Grid & Slices (image 36)

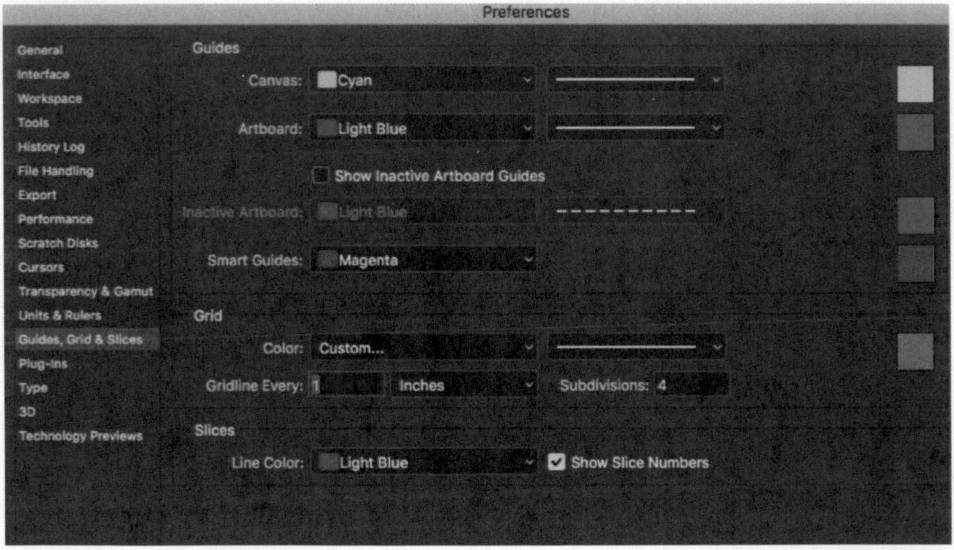

image 36

#32 Switch the "Cancel" button to "Reset" in Adobe Camera Raw

Switching the "Cancel" button to "Reset" helped me a lot. Sometimes after many steps I realized that I am not sure if I like the result so I decided to start all over. To save me time and not exit the Camera Raw filter I switched "Cancel"button to "Reset"
Simply press Option + click on "Cancel" button (Mac) or Alt + click on "Cancel" button (Win)
(images 37 and 37.1)

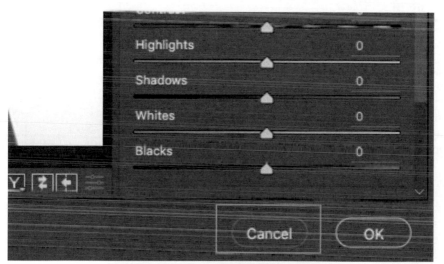

image 37

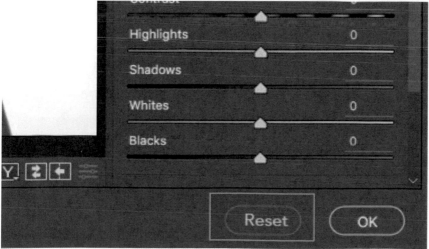

image 37.1

#33 Camera Raw Shortcuts

Reset Camera Raw Preferences:
Command + Option + Shift + double click on raw image (Mac)
Ctrl + Alt + Shift + double click on raw image (Win)

Multiple Undo:
Command + Option + Z (Mac)
Ctrl + Alt + Z (Win)

Multiple Redo:
Command + Shift + Z (Mac)
Ctrl + Shift + Z (Win)

Zoom In:
Command + plus sign (Mac)
Ctrl + plus sign (Win)

Zoom Out:
Command + minus sign (Mac)
Ctrl + minus sign (Win)

Zoom tool 100%:
Command + Option + 0 (zero) (Mac)
Ctrl + Alt + 0 (zero) (Win)

Crop Tool:
C

Hand Tool:
H

Adjustment Brush:
K

White Balance Tool:
I

#34 Open Raw Files in Camera Raw by Default

To setup opening Raw Files in Camera Raw:
Preferences > File Handling > check "Prefer Adobe Camera Raw for Supported Raw Files" box (image 38)

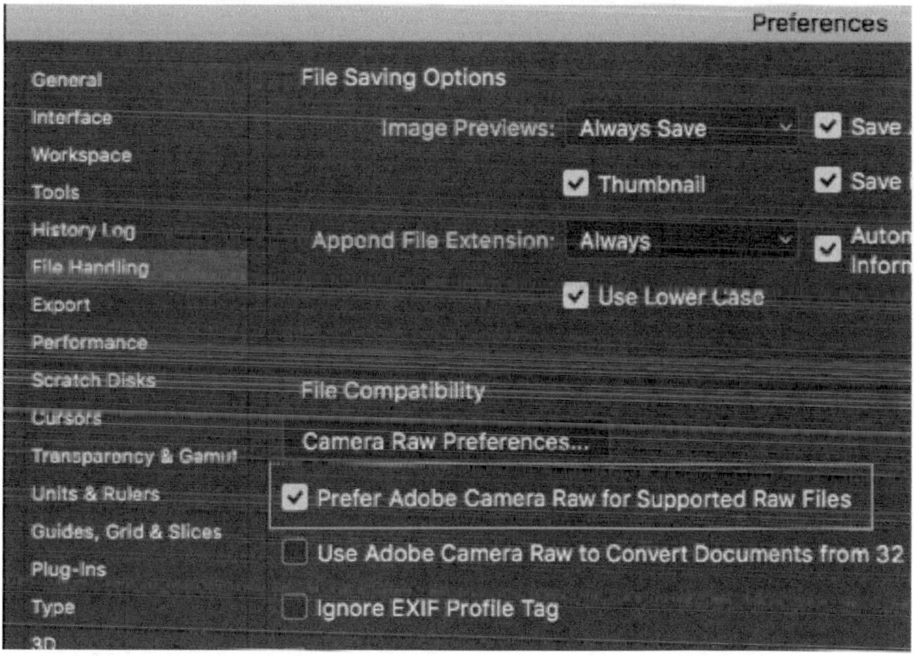

image 38

#35 Multiple Undos

Multiple Undo:
Command + Option + Z (Mac) or
Ctrl + Alt + Z (Win)

#36 Multiple Redos

Multiple Redo:
Command + Shift + Z (Mac) or
Ctrl + Shift + Z (Win)

#37 Camera Raw : Zoom to Fit

Zoom to Fit:
Command + 0 (zero) (Mac) or
Ctrl + 0 (zero) (Win)

#38 Zoom Tool in Adobe Camera Raw

Zoom Tool:
Z

#39 Camera Raw Save Image (bypass dialog box)

Save Image (bypass dialog box):
Command + Option + S (Mac) or
Ctrl + Alt + S (Win)

#40 Full Screen Mode in Adobe Camera Raw

Camera Raw Full Screen Mode:
F

#41 Before and After in Adobe Camera Raw

To preview before and after in Camera Raw:
Q (image 39)

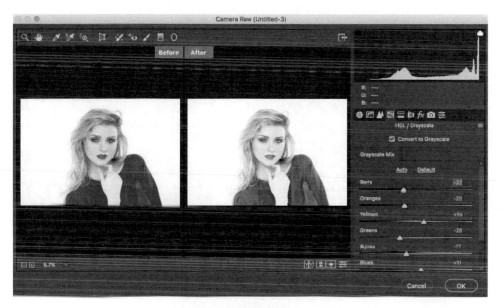

image 39

#42 Preset Panel

To Open Presets panel in Camera Raw:
Command + Option + 9 (Mac) or
Ctrl + Alt + 9 (Win)

#43 Auto Tone Adjustment

To apply Auto Tone Adjustment in Camera Raw:
Command + U (Mac) or
Ctrl + U (Win)

#44 Save Your Settings in Adobe Camera Raw as a Preset

To save your Camera Raw setting as a preset simply:
Choose "Save Settings" from the Camera Raw settings menu (image 40)

image 40

#45 Switch between Horizontal and Vertical Preview

To switch between Horizontal & Vertical preview in Camera Raw simply click "Cycles between Before/After views" (image 41, 42 and 42.1)

image 41

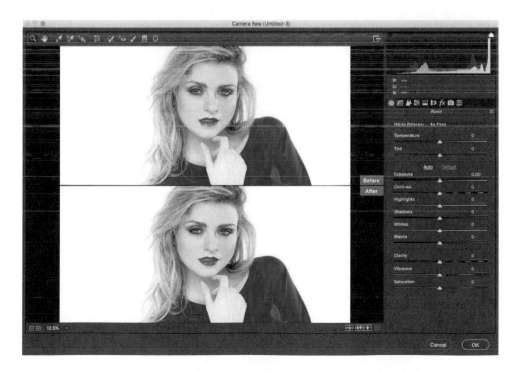

image 42

image 42.1

#46 Setup File Info Templates

I recommend you to spend some time on this topic. File info (metadata) is a very important. The right file info will display all necessary information about the document along with showing your copyright.
Tip: use only fields important for you and your workflow.
Pay close attention to the Copyright info

File > File Info (image 43)

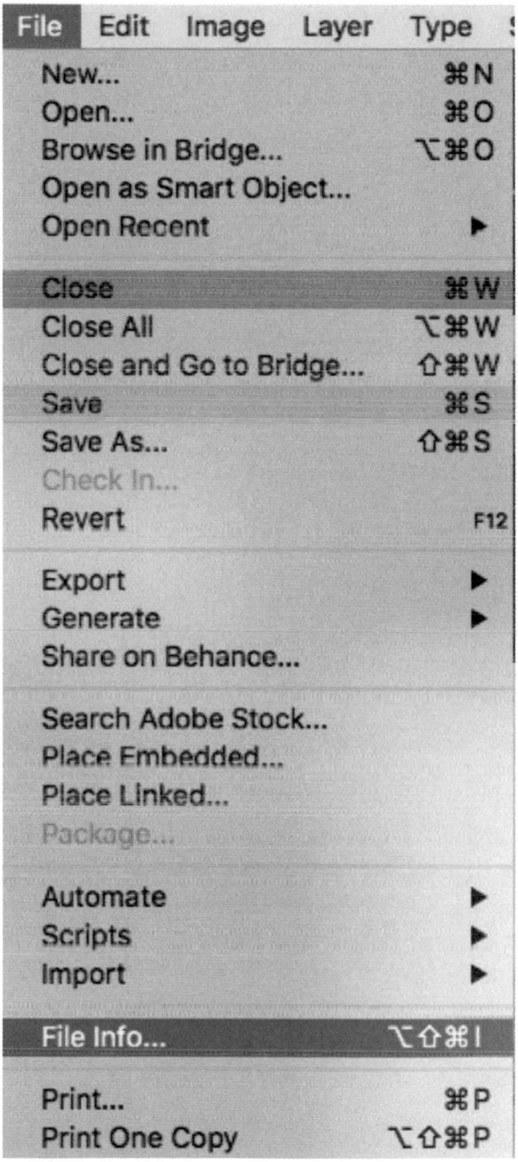
File
Edit
Image
Layer
Type
New... ⌘N
Open... ⌘O
Browse in Bridge... ⌥⌘O
Open as Smart Object...
Open Recent
Close ⌘W
Close All ⌥⌘W
Close and Go to Bridge... ⇧⌘W
Save ⌘S
Save As... ⇧⌘S
Check In...
Revert F12
Export
Generate
Share on Behance...
Search Adobe Stock...
Place Embedded...
Place Linked...
Package...
Automate
Scripts
Import
File Info... ⌥⇧⌘I
Print... ⌘P
Print One Copy ⌥⇧⌘P

image 43

Type all desired information you want to use. I will recommend at least:
Document Title, Author,Keywords,Copyright Status,Copyright Notice (image 44)

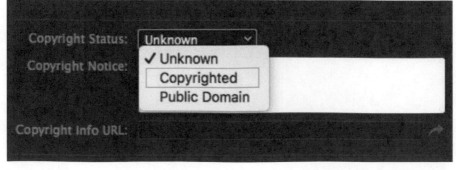

image 44

Especially pay attention to your copyright info (images 45 and 45.1)

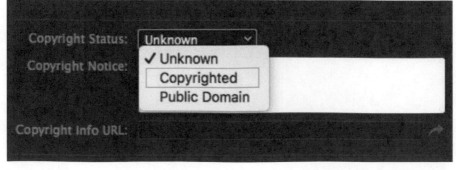

image 45

image 45.1

Save your file info as a template (image 46)

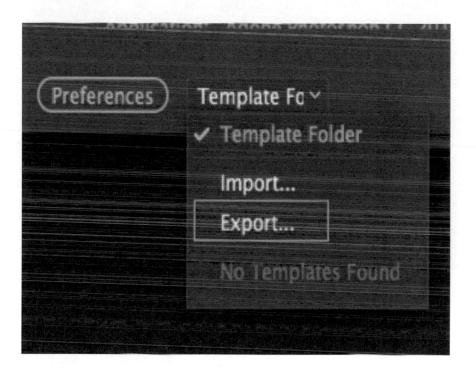

image 46

#47 Convert Layers to Smart Filter Layers

Smart Filters (aka Smart Objects) feature helps you apply filters nondestructively. Once you choose this option your layer or background will be converted into a smart object. Then you can apply any filters you want non-destructively. If you want to remove/adjust a filter later, you can. No pixels will be harmed in this process:
Filter > Convert for Smart Filters (images 47 and 48)

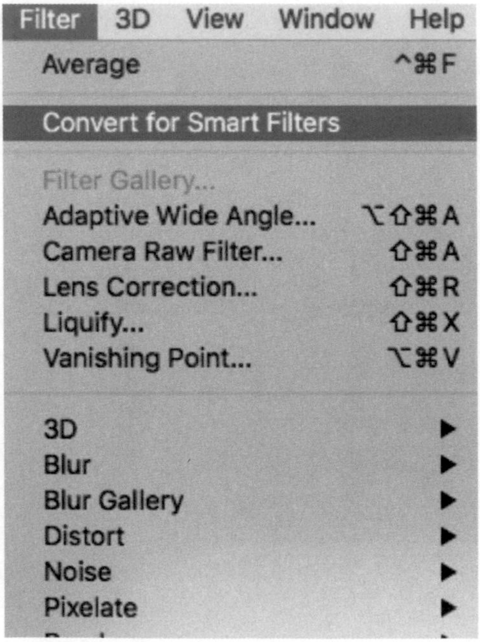

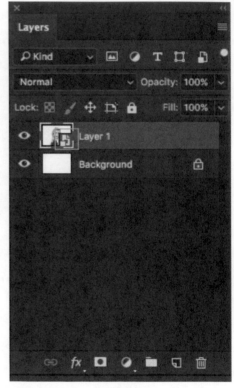

image 47

image 48

After you applied Smart Filters you can edit or delete Smart Filters any time:
Double-click the Smart Filter in the Layer panel to edit its properties (image 49)

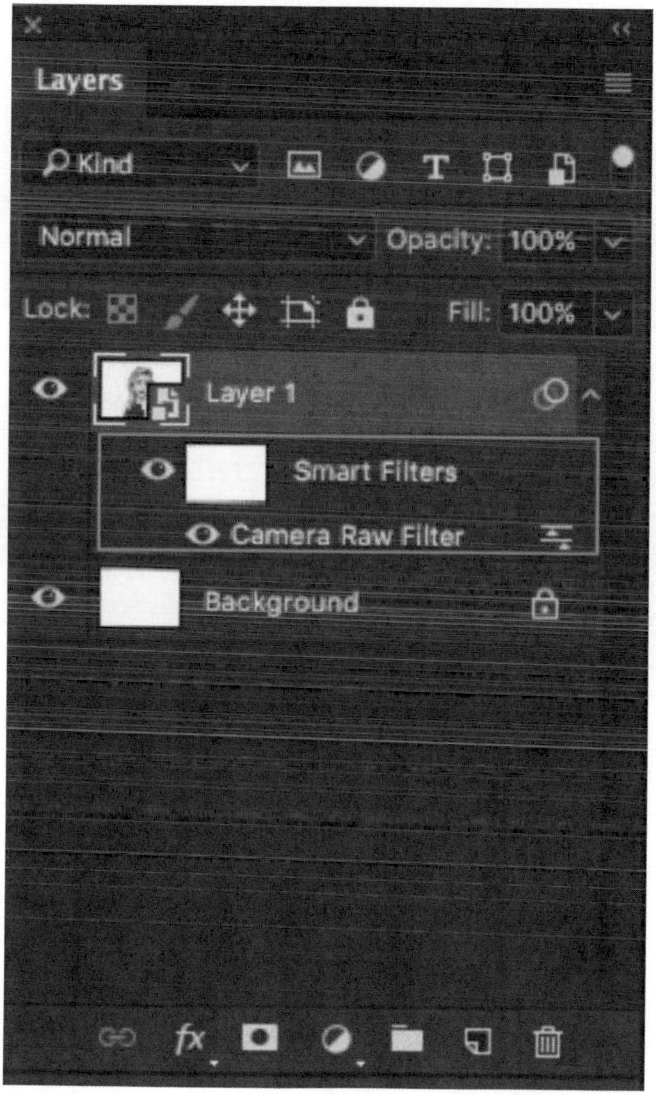

image 49

#48 Face-Aware Liquify Filter

Face-Aware Liquify is one of the best (magical) Adobe Photoshop Features. Face-Aware Liquify automatically detects facial features in your image and allows you to adjust them or create something fun.
To access to Face-Aware Liquify:
Filter > Liquify (images 50 and 51)

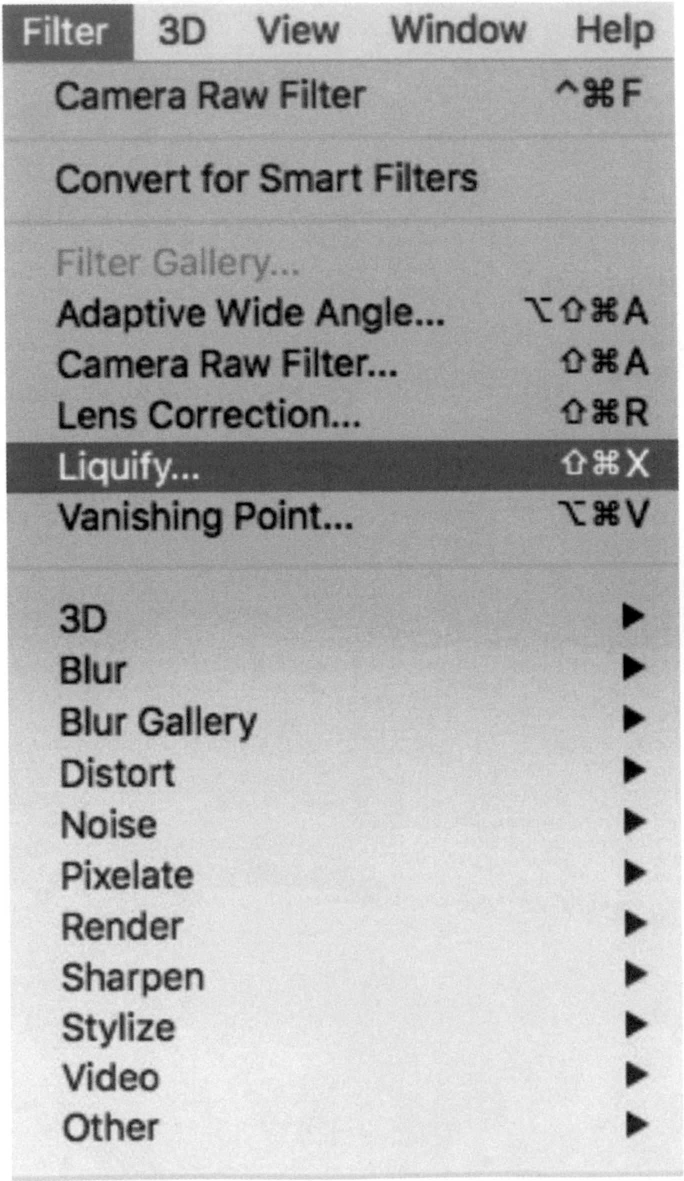

image 50

image 51

Before you will start applying Face-Aware Liquify make sure you checked "Preview" box which will help you to preview result in real time (image 52)

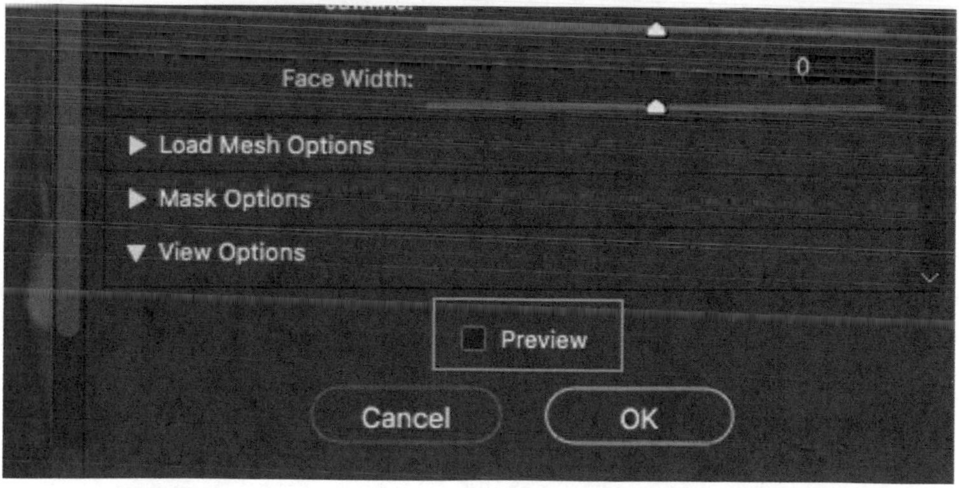

image 52

#49 Symmetrical Adjustment

To apply symmetrical adjustment for both eyes in Face-Aware Liquify click on an link icon between two sliders.(image 53)

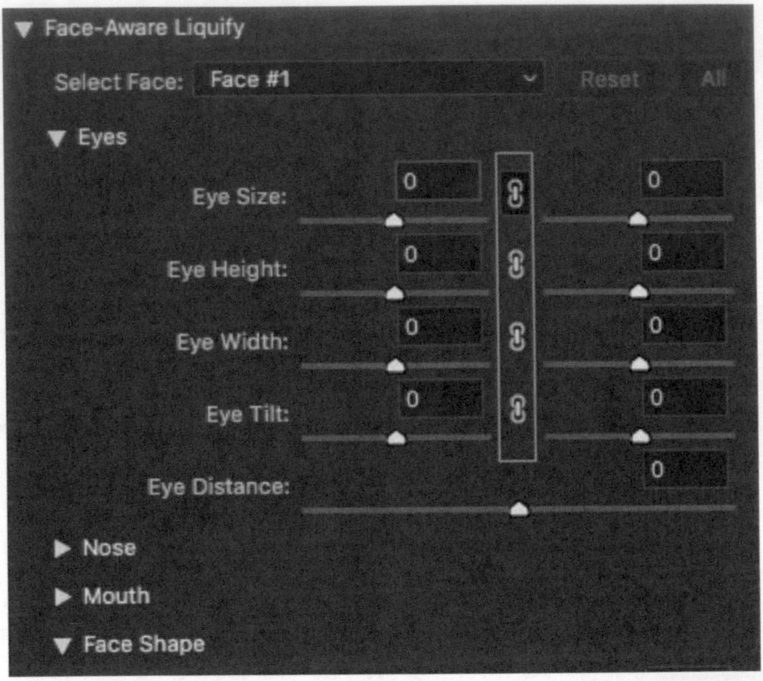

image 53

#50 Apply Adjustments on-image in Face-Aware liquify

If you want to apply Face-Aware Liquify with on-image controls, check "Show Face Overlay" box. With Show Face Overlay checked box you will be able to see all handles around facial features such as nose, eyes, mouth,and face shape (image 54)

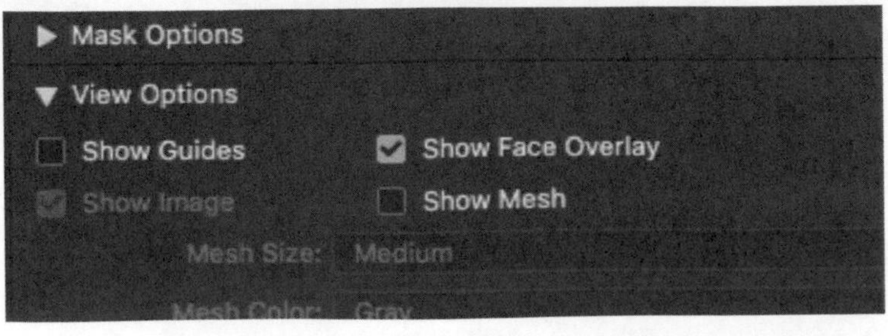

image 54

#51 Show Before/After in Face-Aware liquify

To show before/after in Face-Aware Liquify check "Show Backdrop" box (image 55)

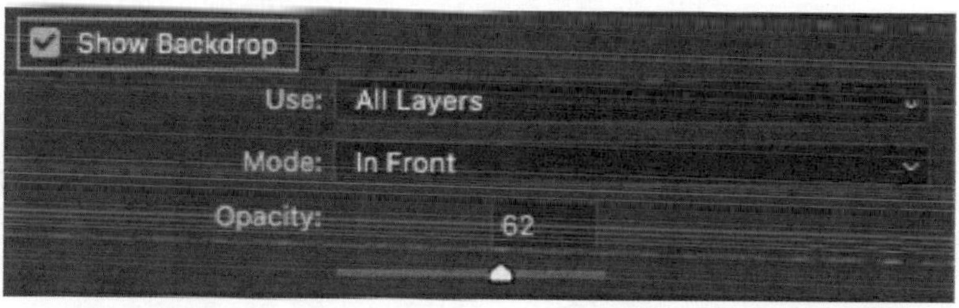

image 55

#52 Switch between faces

If you have two or more faces in your image you can adjust them individually and switch between them. To switch between faces in Face-Aware Liquify choose the face you want to apply adjustments to from "Select Faces" drop down menu (images 56 and 57)

image 56

image 57

#53 Pin Edges in Liquify

Checking the "Pin Edges" box in Liquify helps you to apply Liquify without pulling in the edges of your document in by mistake (image 58)

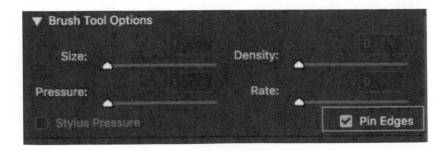

image 58

#54 Switch Cancel to Reset Temporarily

To switch the Cancel button to Reset in Liquify:
Press Option + click on Cancel button (Mac) or Alt + click on Cancel button (Win)

#55 Freeze Mask Tool in Liquify

By freezing areas of your image you will prevent apply any changes to those areas. This is really helpful when you want to liquify something that is close or even touching something else in the photo that you don't want affected.
Using the freeze mask tool simply paint over the area you want to protect against any changes. The temporarily protected area will be in red. (images 59 and 60)

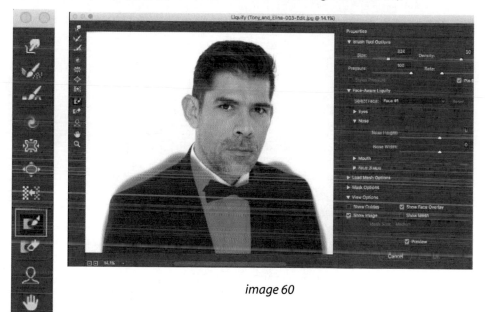

image 60

image 59

Tip: Don't forget to check "Show Mask" box (image 61)

image 61

#56 Use the Tree Filter to Generate Trees

Applying the Tree Filter to a separate Layer lets you generate a tree and then gives you ability to apply any manipulation to it because you created a blank layer first.
To apply a Tree filter as a separate Layer:
Create a new Layer (image 62)

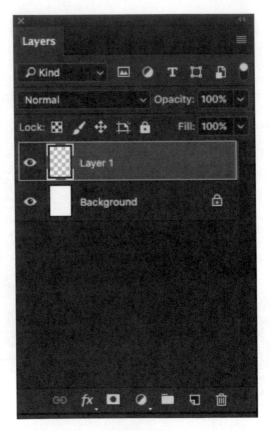

image 62

Filter > Render > Tree (image 63)

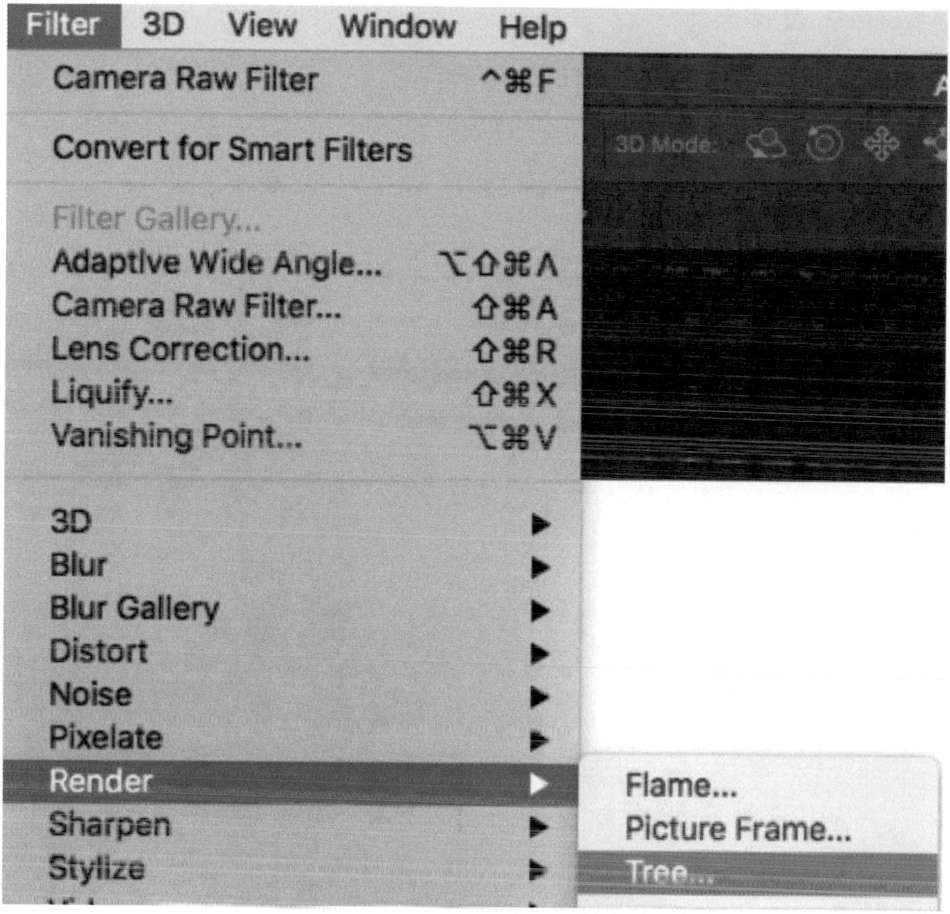

Filter
3D
View
Window
Help
Camera Raw Filter ^⌘F
Convert for Smart Filters
3D Mode:
Filter Gallery...
Adaptive Wide Angle... ⌥⇧⌘A
Camera Raw Filter... ⇧⌘A
Lens Correction... ⇧⌘R
Liquify... ⇧⌘X
Vanishing Point... ⌥⌘V
3D
Blur
Blur Gallery
Distort
Noise
Pixelate
Render
Sharpen
Stylize
Flame...
Picture Frame...
Tree...

image 63

The Tree filter will be applied as a separate layer (image 64)

image 64

#57 Use Adjustments Layers

Applying Adjustments as a separate Layers give you flexibility to work with Adjustment Layer later on at any time
non-destructively.
Window > Adjustments (image 64)

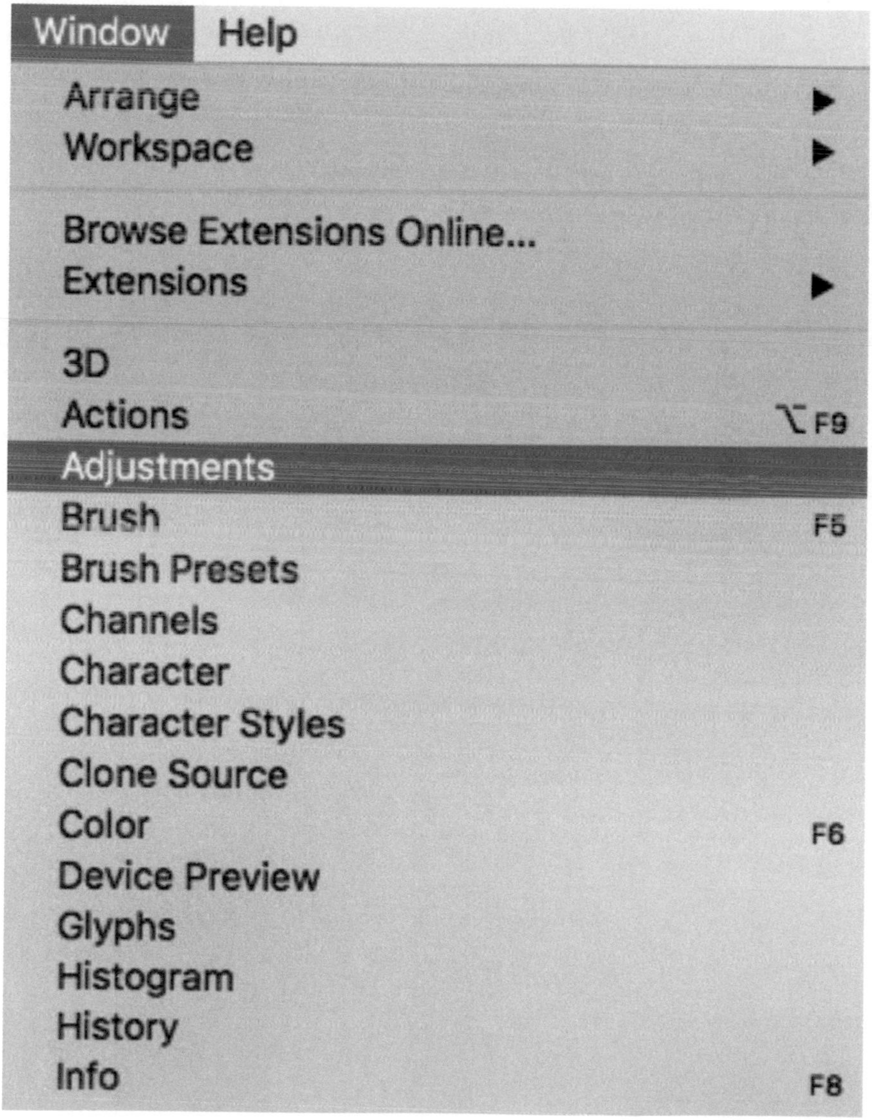

Window   Help
   Arrange ▶
   Workspace ▶

   Browse Extensions Online...
   Extensions ▶

   3D
   Actions ⌥F9
   Adjustments
   Brush F5
   Brush Presets
   Channels
   Character
   Character Styles
   Clone Source
   Color F6
   Device Preview
   Glyphs
   Histogram
   History
   Info F8

image 64

Adjustment will be applied as a separate layer and you can apply any modification or delete this Layer at any time (image 66)

image 66

#58 Convert the Background to a Layer with a Single Click

To unlock background only with one click:
Click on lock icon (image 67)

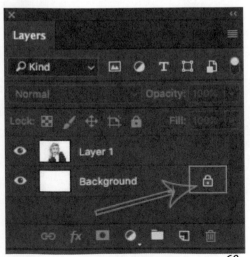

image 67

#59 Customize Menus

To customize menus:
Edit > Menus (images 68 and 69)

image 68

Keyboard Shortcuts   Menus

Menu For: Application Menus   ∨   Set: Photoshop Defaults (modified) ∨

OK

Cancel

Application Menu Command	Visibility	Color
New...	👁	None
Open...	👁	None
Browse in Bridge...	👁	None
Open as Smart Object...	👁	None
Open Recent>	👁	None
Clear Recent File List		None
Close		Red
Close All	👁	None

ⓘ To hide menu items, click on the Visibility button.
Show All Menu Items will be appended to the bottom of a menu that contains hidden items.
To temporarily see hidden menu items, click on Show All Menu Items or ⌘ + click on the menu.
To add color to a menu item, click in the Color column.
To turn off menu colors, go to the Interface Preference panel and uncheck Show Menu Colors.

image 69

#60 Make the Color Panel Longer

Arranging your workspace can be very helpful. I prefer to have my panels that I work with the most opened and arranged by priority and also by size. I make the color panel as long as possible and have it open all the times. (image 70)

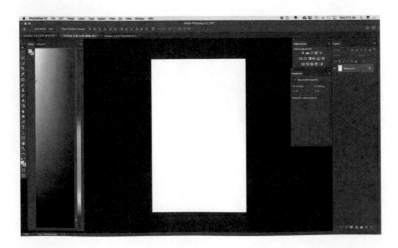

image 70

To open Color panel:
Window > Color (image 71)

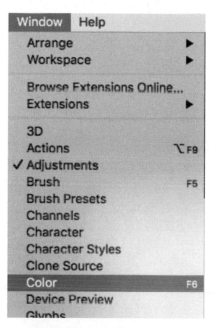

image 71

To make Color panel longer simply point your mouse cursor to the bottom edge of the panel and when your cursor changes into an up and down pointing arrow simply click and drag downward to resize it. (image 72)

image 72

#61 Add Your Own Custom Keyboard Shortcuts

To create your own custom Photoshop keyboard shortcuts:
Edit > Keyboard Shortcuts (images 73 and 74)

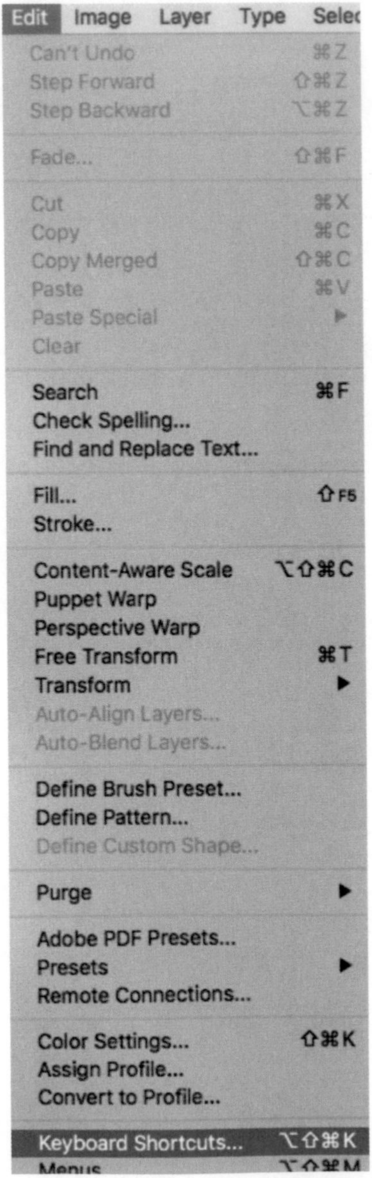

image 73

image 74

Choose which shortcut set you want to make changes to (image 75)

image 75

And now you will be able to change or add the keyboard shortcuts you want. Keep in mind that in many cases the keyboard shortcut you want to use is already used for something else. You can make your own set and override any existing keyboard shortcut to be whatever you want.(image 76)

image 76

#62 Custom Foreground and Background colors

To change background or foreground color to any color from your active document: Pick Eyedropper tool from toolbar (image 77)

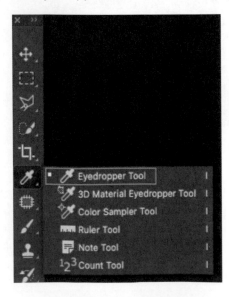

image 77

Click on the color in the active document you want to use (image 78)

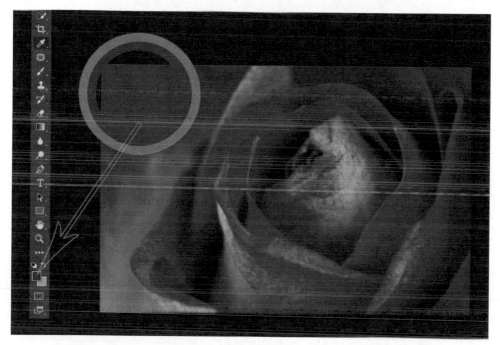

image 78

#63 Default Background/Foreground colors

To switch to default Foreground/Background (Black and White) colors in Photoshop simply press "D" on your keyboard. Tip: Pressing "x" on the keyboard will toggle them back and forth.

#64 List of Most Recently Used Brushes

To see the list of most recently used brushes:
Open brush Preset Panel and you will see the list of most recently used brushes on a top row of the panel (image 79)

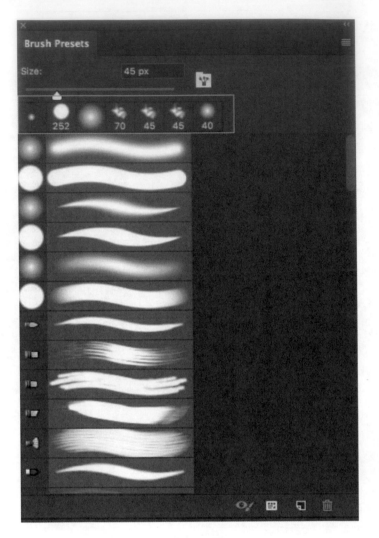

image 79

#65 Recently Used Colors

To see the recent used colors:
Window > Swatches (image 80)

Window	Help	
Arrange	▶	
Workspace	▶	
Browse Extensions Online...		
Extensions	▶	
3D		
Actions	⌥F9	
✓ Adjustments		
Brush	F5	
Brush Presets		
Channels		
Character		
Character Styles		
Clone Source		
Color	F6	
Device Preview		
Glyphs		
Histogram		
History		
Info	F8	
Layer Comps		
✓ Layers	F7	
✓ Libraries		
Measurement Log		
Navigator		
Notes		
Paragraph		
Paragraph Styles		
Paths		
Properties		
Styles		
Swatches		
Timeline		
Tool Presets		

image 80

You can preview the most recently used color on a top row of swatches panel (image 81)

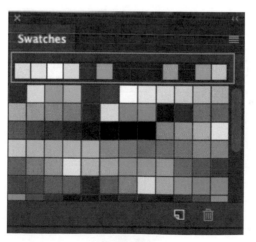

image 81

69

#66 Reset a Photoshop Tool

To reset a tool:
Select a tool you want to reset > Tool Preset > Reset Tool (image 82)

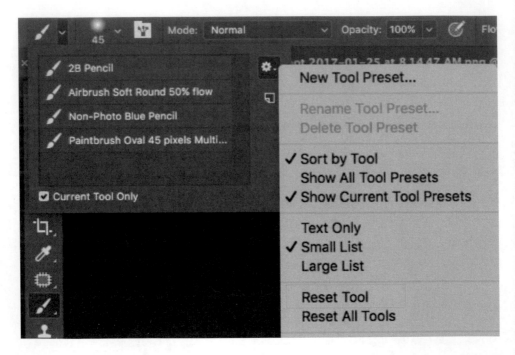

image 82

#67 Layer's Panel Thumbnail Size

You can change Layer's panel thumbnail size directly from layer panel. Tip: make your thumbnail size small when you are working with several layers (images 83 and 84)

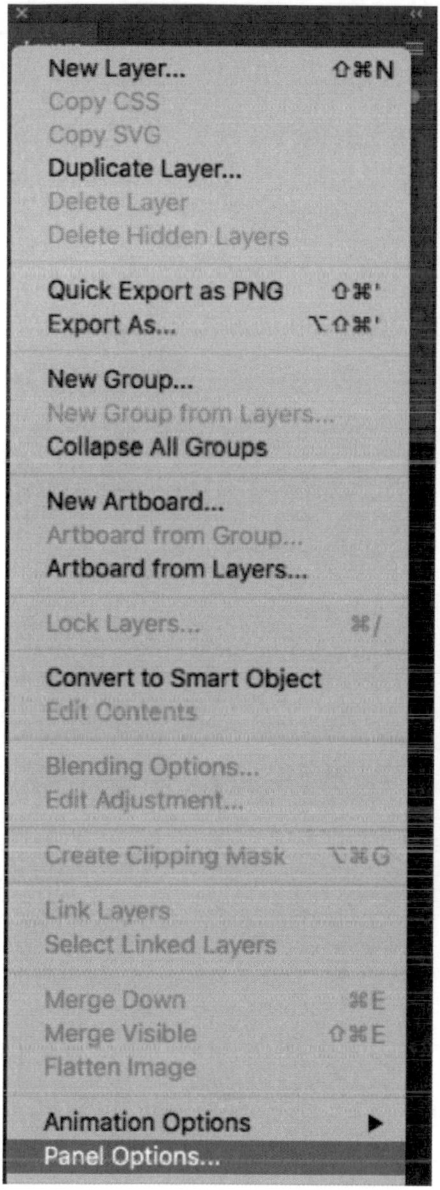

image 83

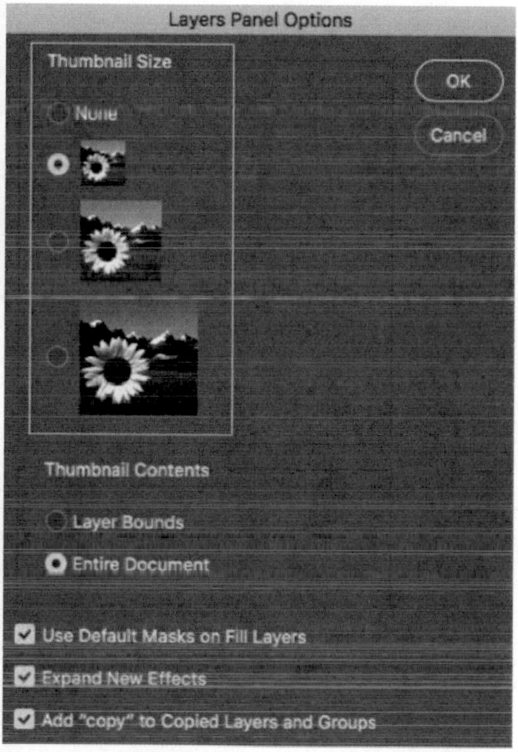

image 84

#68 Text and Properties Panel

Now you can apply modification to your text Layer directly from Properties Panel:
Type your text (image 85)

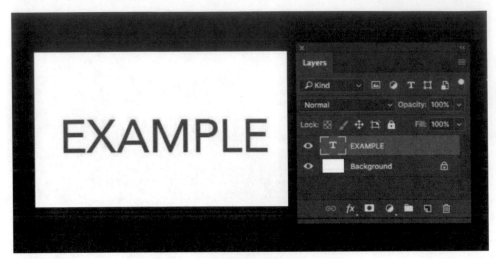

image 85

Open Properties panel:
Window > Properties (image 86)

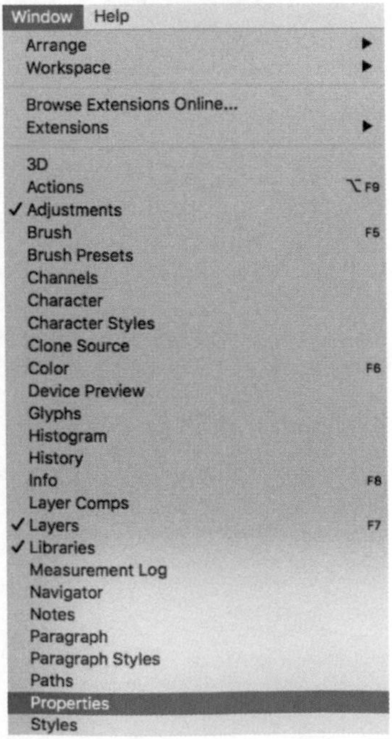

image 86

And now you can apply any changes to your text Layer directly from properties panel (image 87)

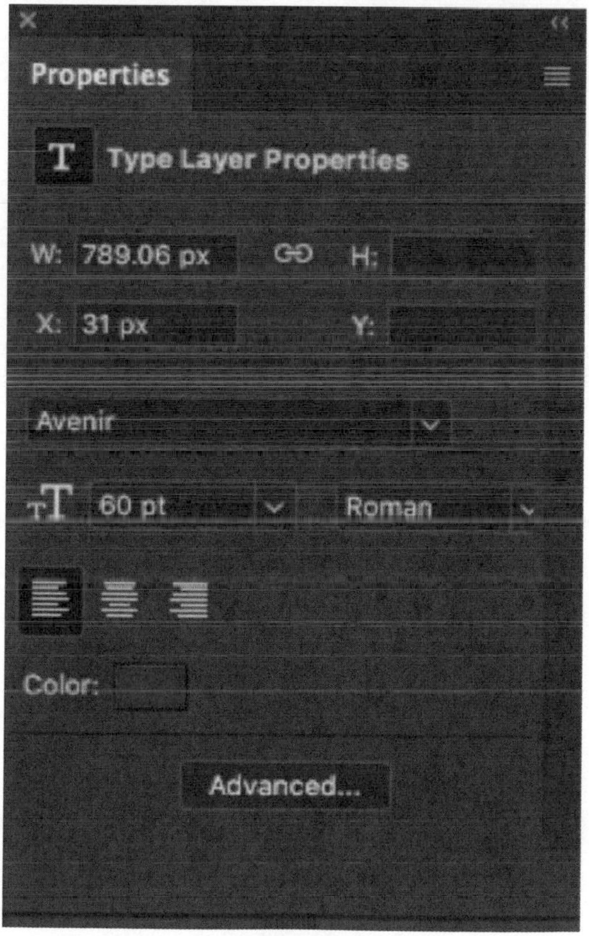

image 87

#69 Shape Properties

You can change the shape properties directly form the Properties panel:
Create a shape (image 88)

image 88

Window > Properties (image 89)

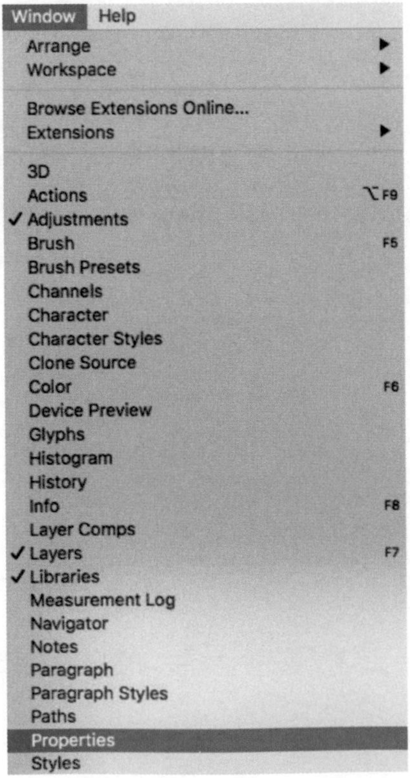

image 89

Apply any modification to your shape directly from the Properties panel (image 90)

image 90

#70 Few More Keyboard Shortcuts

Step Backward (Undo):
Command + Option + Z (Mac) Control + Alt + Z (Win)

Step Forward (Redo):
Command + Shift + Z (Mac) Control + Shift + Z (Win)

Add to a Selection:
Selection Tool + Shift- drag (Mac) Selection Tool + Shift -drag (Win)

Subtract from a Selection:
Selection Tool + Option-drag (Mac) Selection Tool + Alt -drag

#71 Creating a Clipping Mask

To create a Clipping Mask:
Press Option (Mac) or Alt (Win) > position your mouse between two layers (right on the line that separates the two layers) and click (images 91 and 92)

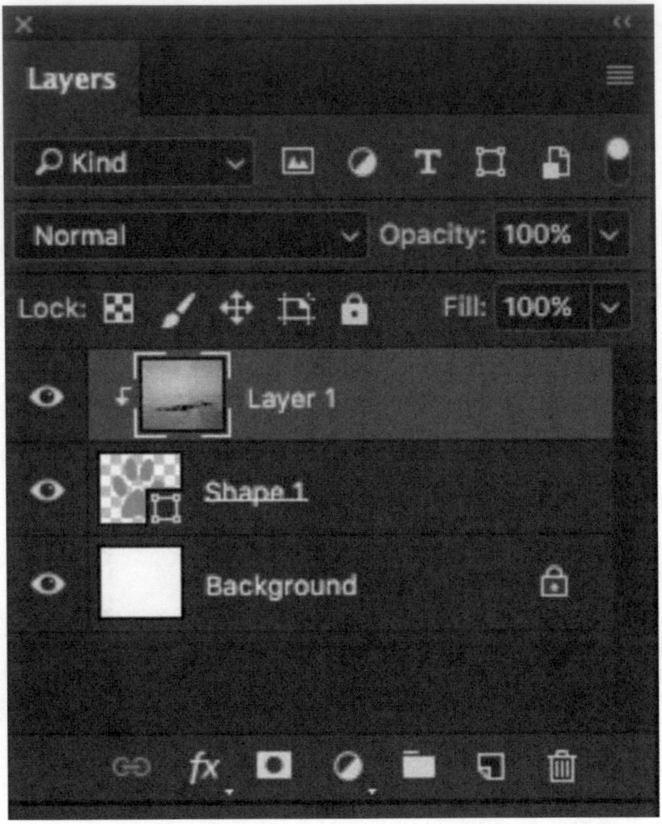

image 91

Tip: To create a clipping mask you can use keyboard shortcut as well
Command + Option + G (Mac) or Ctrl + Alt + G (Win)

image 92

#72 Camera Raw in Full Screen

To expend Camera Raw in full screen simply click on "Toggle full screen mode" icon or just press "F"
(image 93)

image 93

#73 ESC key to Commit Text

I found it very beneficial to setup the ESC key to commit text.
Preferences > Type (image 94) Tip: Now in Photoshop CC you can also click outside the text frame to commit the text.

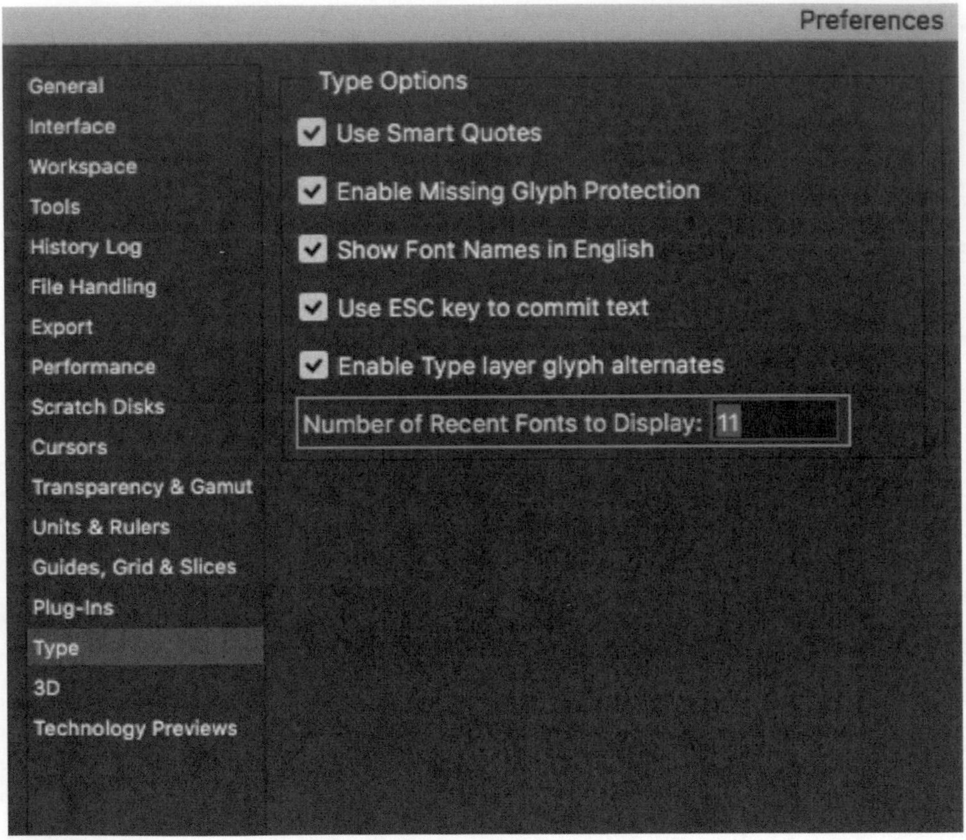

image 94

#74 Specify number of recently used fonts to display

To specify number of recent fonts to display simply type the number in "Number of Recent Font to Display"
(images 95 and 96)

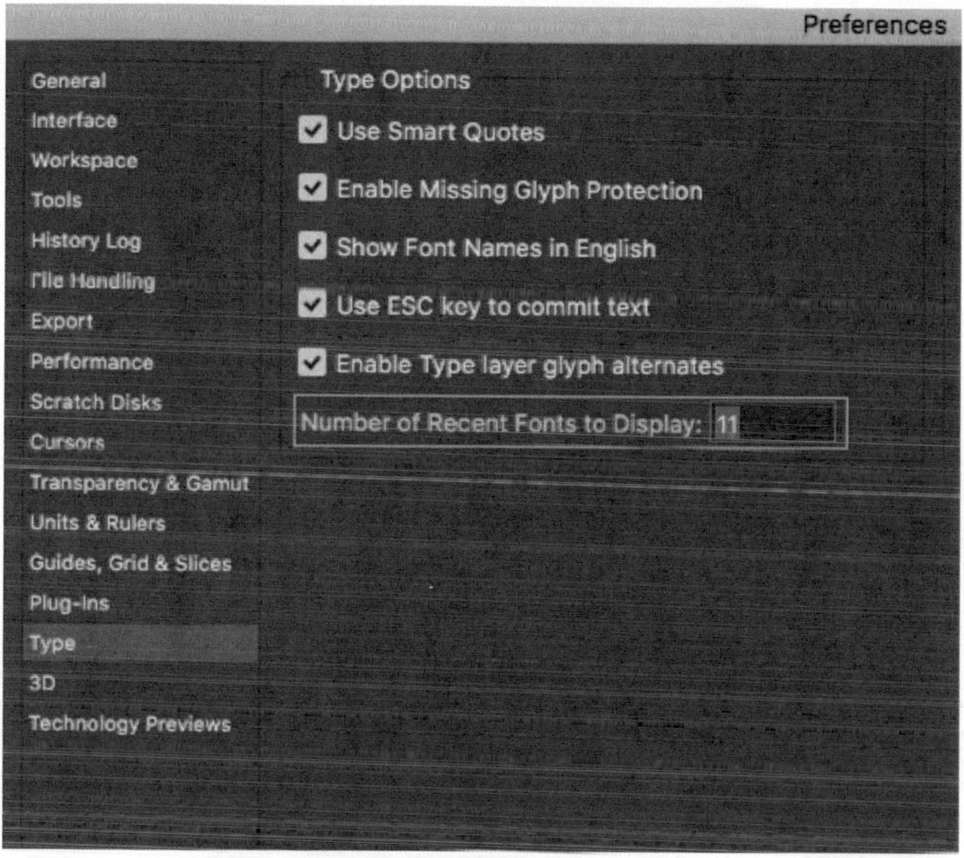

image 95

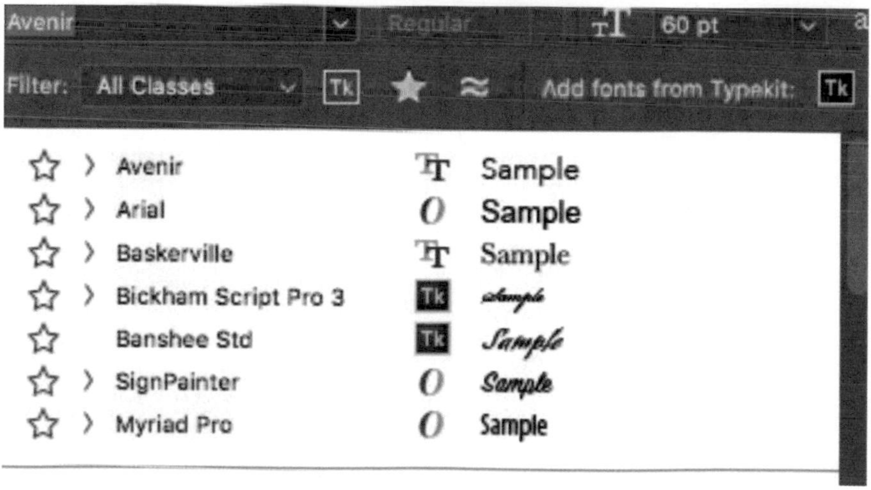

image 96

#75 Show the Start Workspace

Start workspace allows to quickly access to recent files, CC files, search for assets in Adobe Stock. To enable "Show Start Workspace When No Documents Are Open": Preferences > General > check "Show "Start" Workspace When No Documents Are Open" box (image 97)

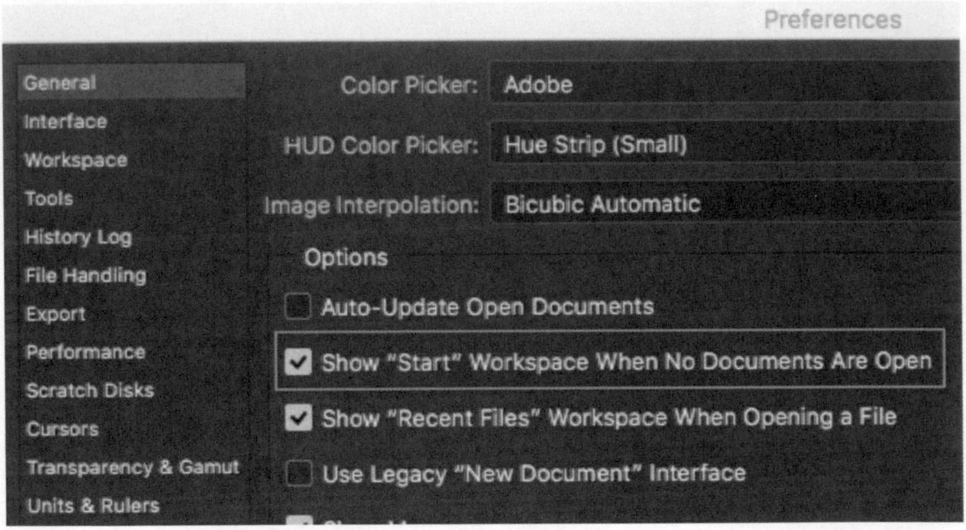

image 97

#76 Show/Hide Recent Files

"Show Recent Files" feature saved me a lot of time.
Preferences > general > check "Show "Recent Files" Workspace When Opening a File" box (image 98)

Preferences

General	Color Picker: Adobe
Interface	
Workspace	HUD Color Picker: Hue Strip (Small)
Tools	
History Log	Image Interpolation: Bicubic Automatic
File Handling	Options
Export	☐ Auto-Update Open Documents
Performance	
Scratch Disks	☑ Show "Start" Workspace When No Documents Are Open
Cursors	☑ Show "Recent Files" Workspace When Opening a File
Transparency & Gamut	
Units & Rulers	☐ Use Legacy "New Document" Interface
Guides, Grid & Slices	☑ Show Messages
Plug-Ins	ⓘ Workspace changes will take effect th
Type	
3D	
Technology Previews	Reset All Warning Dialogs Res

image 98

#77 Full Screen/Hide all Menus

To hide all menus simply press "F"

#78 Search for the Photoshop Feature You Want Right In Photoshop

You can now search right inside Photoshop for tools, panels, filters, and Adobe Stock right inside Photoshop.
Command + F (Mac) or Ctrl + F (Win) (image 99)

image 99

#79 Camera Raw supports pressure-sensitive Devices

Now Adobe Camera Raw provides support for pressure-sensitive devices such as Wacom, Microsoft Surface Pro tablets.
Pressure applied to the pen will affects the Flow slider within Local Adjustment Brush (image 100)

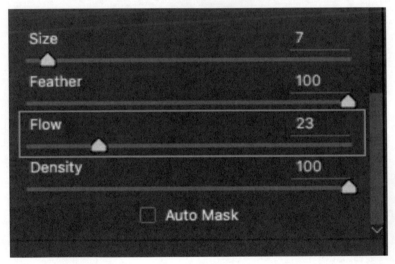

image 100

#80 Select and Mask Workspace

To quickly access to Select and Mask Workspace simply:
Press Command + Option + R (Mac) or Ctrl + Alt + R (Win) (image 101)

image 101

#81 Select and Mask Workspace: Transparency/ Opacity

In Select and Mask Workspace I prefer to use Onion Skin as a View Mode. Onion Skin helps me to preview my selected and background Layers (image 102)

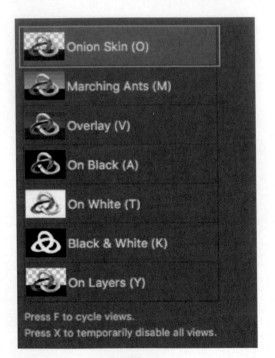

image 102

You can control transparency using "Transparency" slider (image 103)

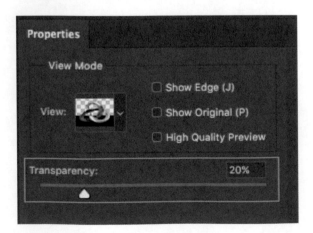

image 103

#82 Artboard Custom Colors

You can apply custom colors to Artboard:
Preferences > Guides,Grid & Slices (image 104)

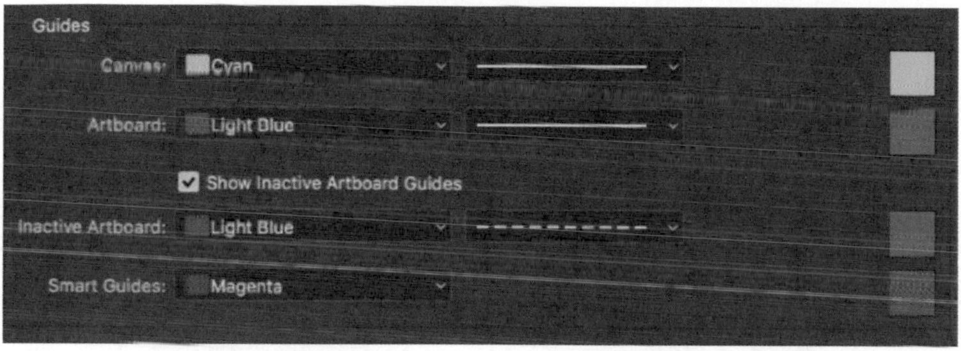

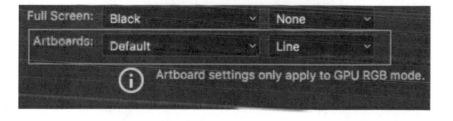

image 104

#83 Artboard Interface Preferences

You can customize Artboard look:
Preferences > Interface > Artboards (image 105)
Tip: Artboard settings only apply to GPU RGB mode

image 105

#84 Create a group from Selected Layers

To create a group from your selected Layers:
Select the Layers you want to create a group from and Click on the Group icon (image 106)

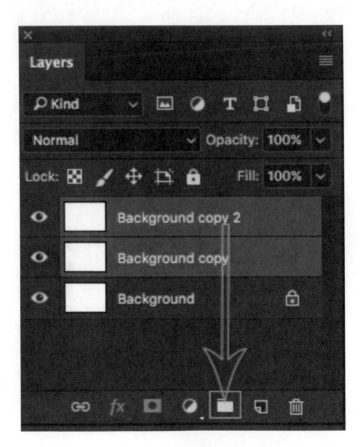

image 106

#85 Disable The Start Window

To Disable the Start Window:
Preferences > General > uncheck "Show "Start" Workspace When No Documents Are Open" (image 107)

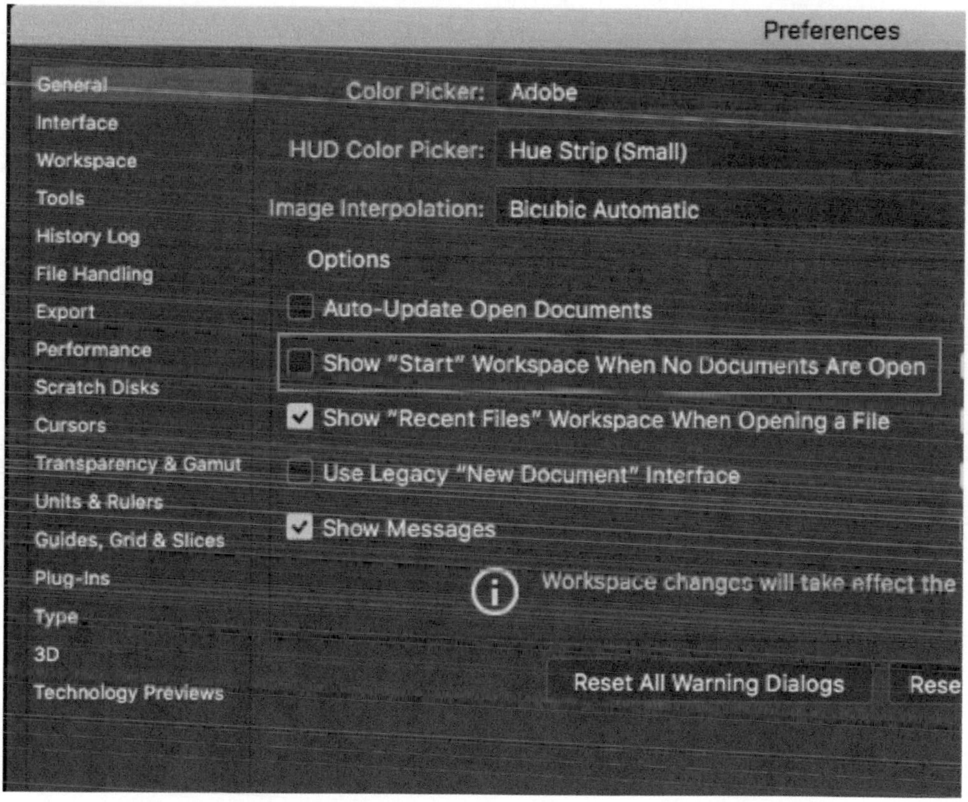

image 107

#86 Adobe Generator

Adobe generator allows you to create image assets in real time. Once you enable it for the document you're working on you can simply add a file extension to the name of layer (or layer group) and Photoshop will create a JPG,PNG or GIF in an assets folder with the same name as your document in the same saved location as your document. As you make changes to the layer/group new images will automatically be generated replacing the old ones.
To turn on Adobe Generator functionality:
File > Generate > Image Assets (image 108)

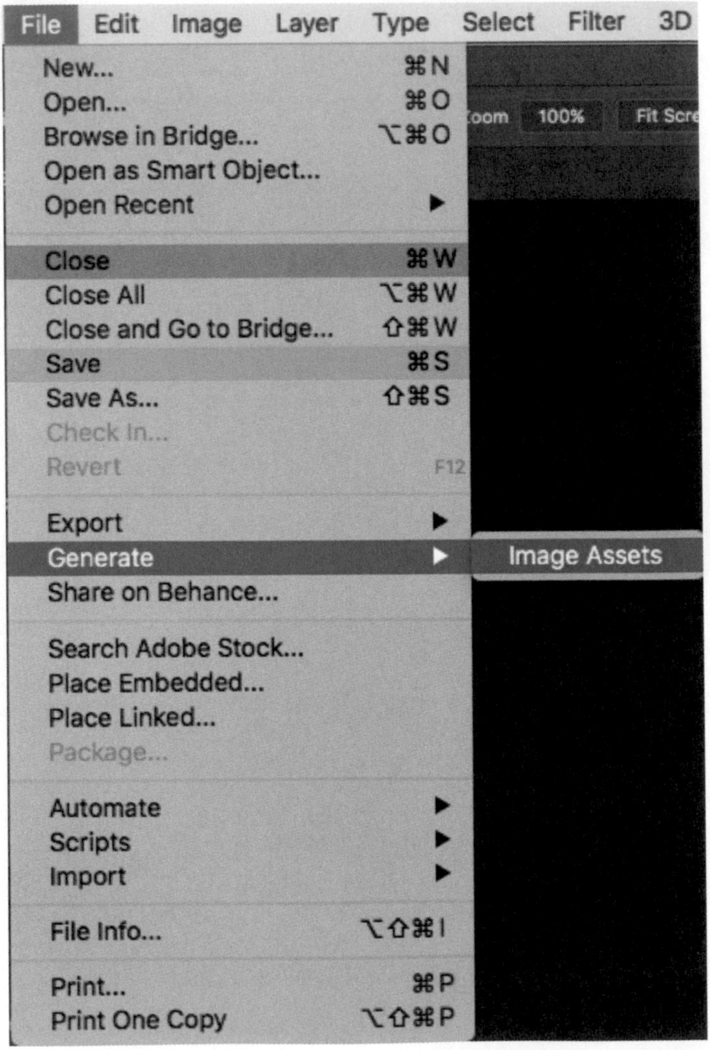

image 108

#87 Customize Your Toolbar

I customize my toolbar for each workflow. I use different tools (more or less) in each workflow so I customized my toolbar in a way to make my workflow easier and faster. Most importantly I can hide tools that I never use.
To customize toolbar:
Edit > Toolbar (images 109 and 110)

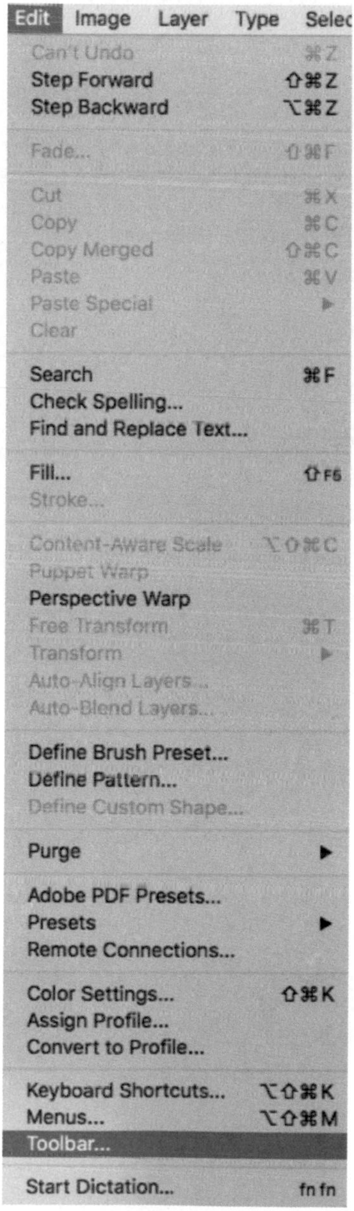

image 109

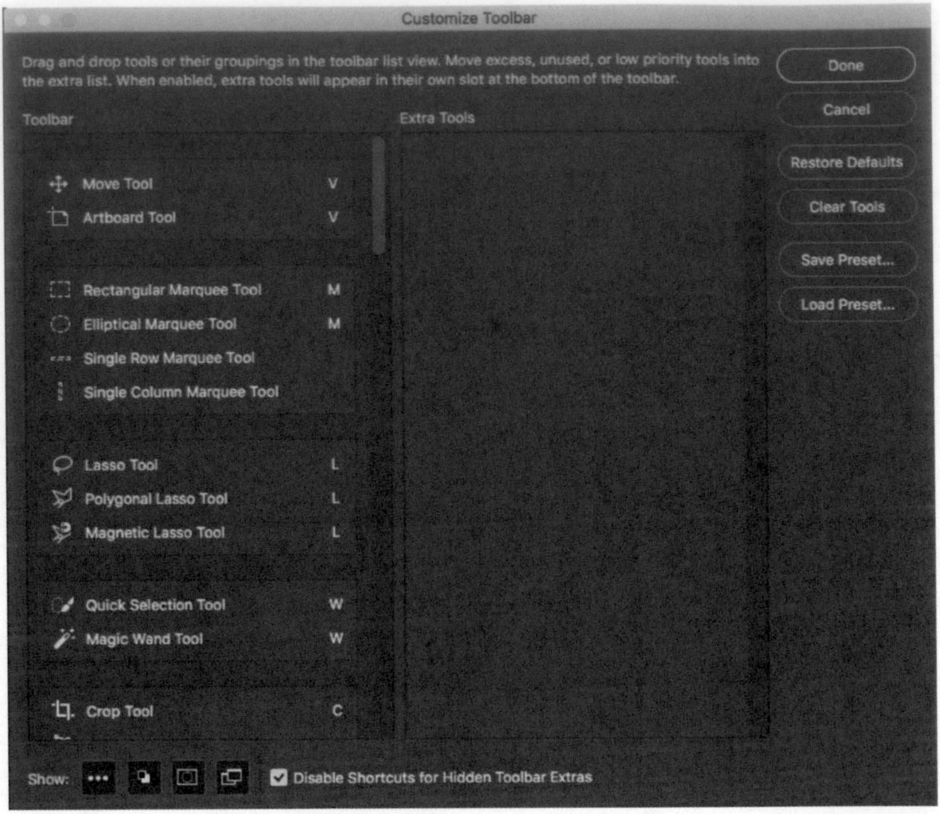

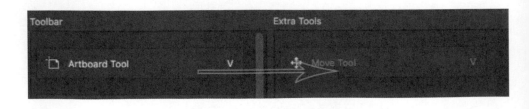

image 110

To remove any tool from toolbar simply click on a tool in "toolbar" side and drag to :Extra Tool" side

image 111

You can restore toolbar at any time simply clicking on Restore Defaults (image 112)

image 112

#88 Hide all Panels and Tools

To hide all Tools and panels
Make sure you're NOT in the Type tool and then Press > Tab on the keyboard. (image 113) Tip: Combine Command/Ctrl F and then a Tab to have a true full screen experience. Great for showing clients your work thus far.

![image 113]

image 113

#89 Hide All Panels except Tools and Control Panel

To hide all panels except Tools and Control panel
Press > Shift + Tab (image 114)

image 114

#90 Create a Custom Workspace

Custom workspace helps you to create a custom workspace for each of your workflow.
Also you can assign the keyboard shortcuts to each workspace. Photoshop already
includes a few to get you started.
To create a new custom workspace:
 Window > Workspace > New Workspace (image 115)

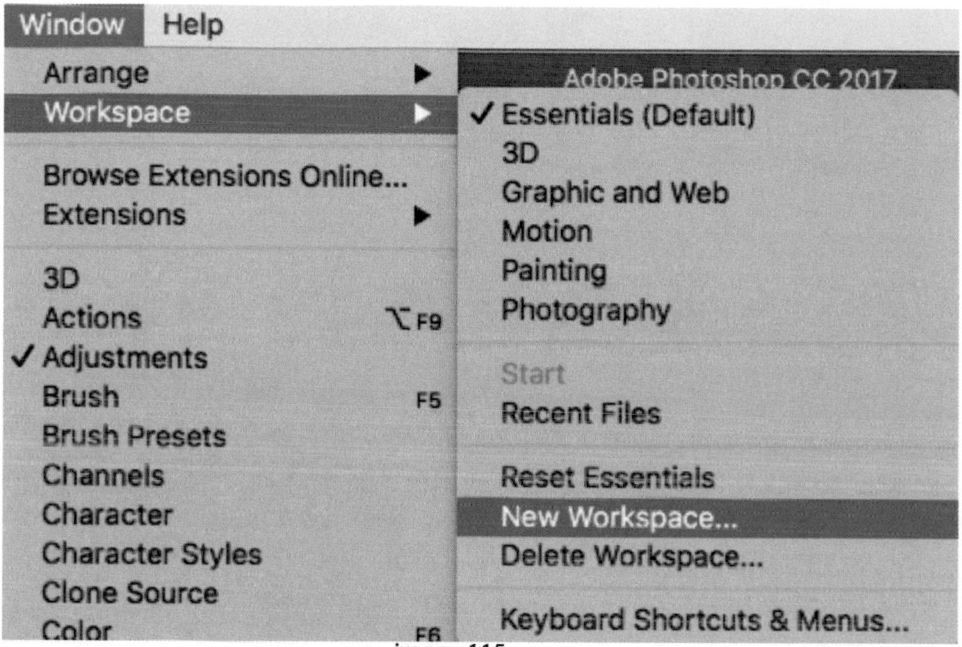

image 115

#91 Delete a Custom Workspace

To delete a custom workspace:
Window > Workspace > Delete Workspace (image 116)

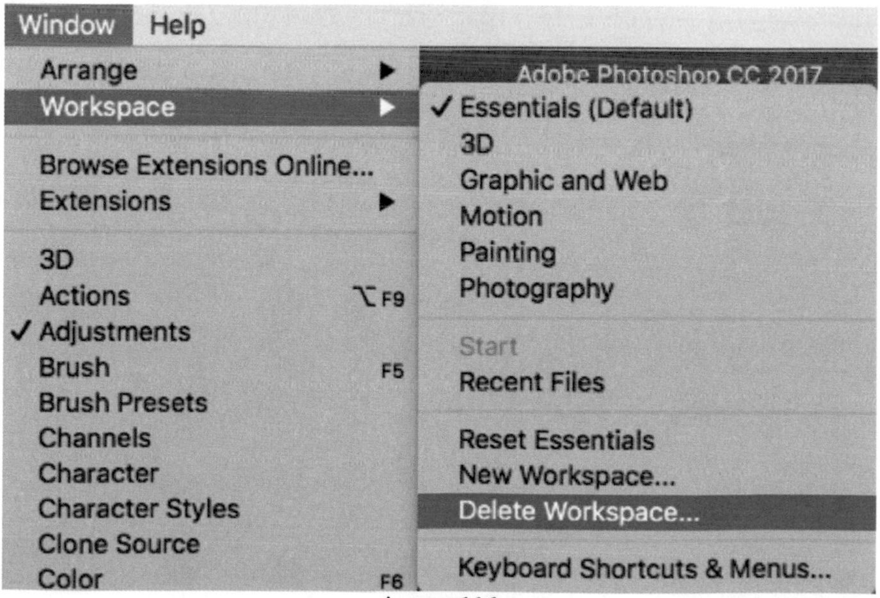

image 116

#92 Restore the Default Workspace

To restore the default workspace:
Window > Workspace > Reset (workspace name) (image 117)

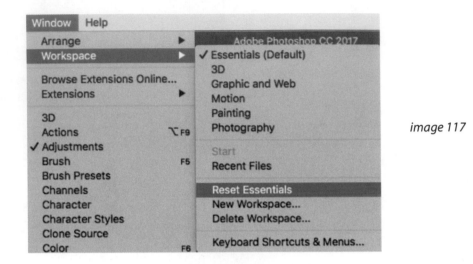

image 117

#93 Create a New Library from Document

For me Libraries is of the most useful features in Adobe Photoshop CC/Creative Cloud. I am using Libraries every day and all day all day long. Photoshop has the unique ability to create a new library from a document. This will take each layer/object, color, style, effect, etc. and put it in a NEW Library.
To create a new Library from document:
Simply click on "New Library from Document" icon (image 118)

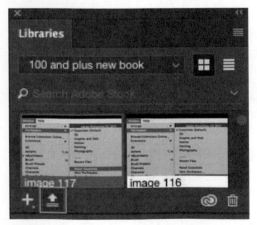

image 118

#94 Search in Library Panel

You can search for Adobe Stock assets directly from Library panel (image 119) Tip: If you use the drop down menu to the right of the search bar you can switch your search to your current library or all libraries.

image 119

#95 View "Deleted" Items

To view deleted items from Library panel:
Click on dropdown menu icon > choose "View Deleted Items" (image 120)

| Create New Library... |
| Create New Library from Document... |
| Collaborate... |
| Share Link... |
| Rename "My Library" |
| Delete "My Library" |
| ✓ Sort by Date |
| Sort by Name |
| View on Website |
| View Deleted Items |
| Learn More |
| Close |
| Close Tab Group |

image 120

#96 Collaboration Directly from the Library Panel

You can invite to collaborate directly from the Library. People that you invite will have full access to the library and they will be able to add/change/delete items. You'll also have the option to just send a link (a copy) of the library so that they can't affect your items:

Click on drop down menu > choose "Collaborate" (image 121)

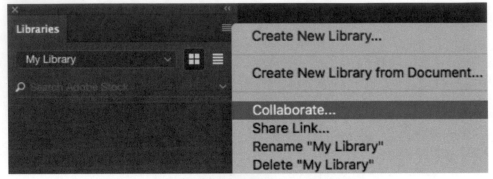

image 121

#97 Save "Save for Web" Settings

If you use Save for Web and you're tired of having to enter your settings every time, this will help you. To save "Save for Web" settings:

Click on dropdown menu > choose Save Settings (images 122 and 122.1)

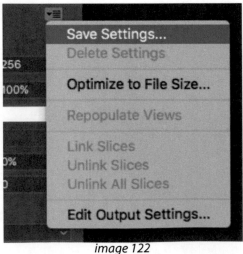

image 122

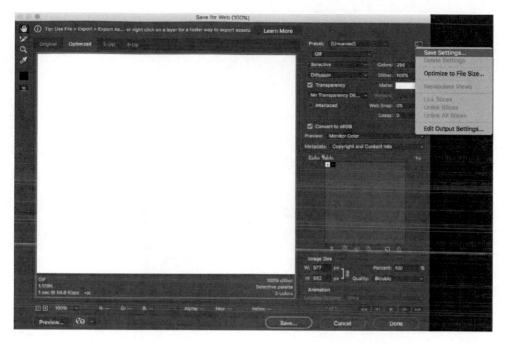

image 122.1

#98 Add Content Directly from the Document to the Library

You can add things to a library from your Photoshop document by dragging them in or you add specific items like this; To add content from the document to the library: Click on "Add Content" sign (image 123)

image 123

Check box next to content you want to add to the library > click on "Add" (image 124)

image 124

#99 Change Content name Directly in a Library Panel

To change content's name directly in a library panel simply double click on a content's name and change it (image 125)

image 125

#100 Package Command

Package Command is a very helpful if you want to send your document to someone with all source file(s) for linked Smart Objects layers.
File > Package (image 128)

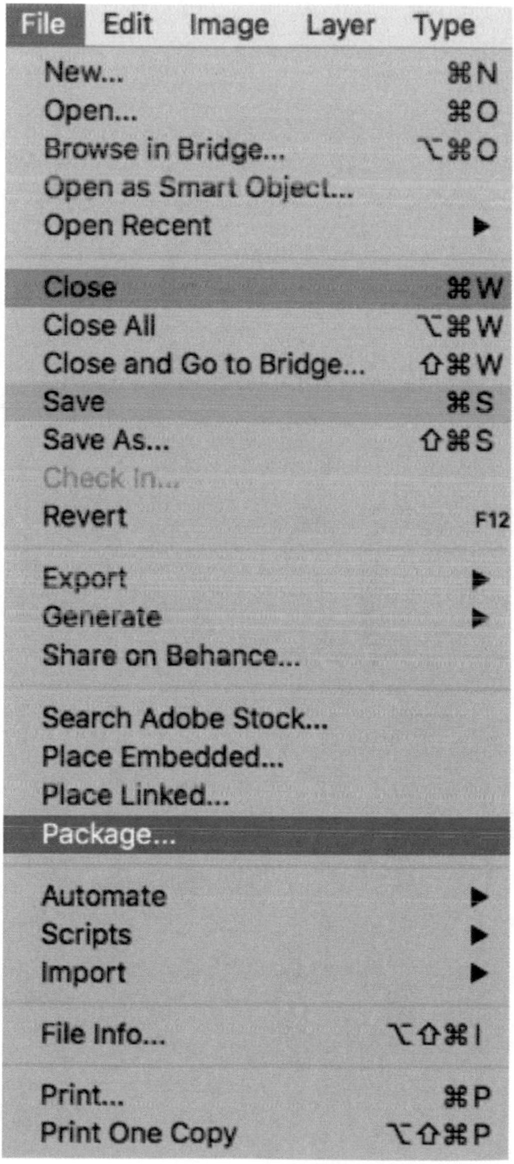

image 128

#101 Change Glyphs with a Single Click

One of the cool things in Photoshop CC is now you have the Glyphs panel (which you can get to from the Window menu). However, one of the coolest features is the ability to use Alternate Glyphs and you can do that without even going to the panel. As long as your Open Type font has alternate glyphs for the character you want to change it will now display those alternates if you just highlight the character on the canvas. You can then just click on the alternate you wish to use. One of my favorite fonts for this is Bickham Script Pro 3. Tip as a Creative Cloud member if your plan allows you access to Typekit fonts you can sync Bickham Script Pro 3 at no additional charge. Just click the Tk button in the font menu on the Control Panel to get to the Typekit website. Do a search for Bickham Script and then sync it to your desktop.

Thank you for buying my book!

48564358R00062

Made in the USA
Middletown, DE
14 June 2019